SELLING WITH STORY

How To Use Storytelling
To Become An Authority, Boost
Sales, And Win The Hearts And
Minds Of Your Audience

Kyle Gray

Don't forget to claim the templates and downloads that go with this book!

To help you put many of the ideas in the book into practice quickly, I have created some easy-to-use templates. They're free to download and modify to fit your needs.

Grab them at
resources.sellingwithstory.co

CONTENTS

FOREWORD BY
JAMES SCHRAMKO

Founder of SuperFastBusiness and Author of *Work Less, Make More.*

It's 8:33 AM; my morning reading is the graffiti on the wall of the surf club toilets.

This was not my usual morning ritual, but I found myself here in the public toilet on the beach. Thankfully, they were open very early in the morning, but I was also annoyed that I had to leave my comfortable house to take care of my morning duty. I probably should've seen this coming; my kid stuffed some paper towels down the toilet (the only one in my apartment) the night before. I paid dearly for it, literally running down the street to get to the surf club just in time. I can laugh about it now, but it was not my favorite moment.

An important idea occurred to me sitting there on that public toilet. I thought about the dozens of business owners that today find themselves in frustrating situations much worse than mine. Sometimes there are challenges you can anticipate, sometimes there are not (like in my case). What's important is setting up your business to run efficiently and predictably whether you're at your best or worst.

Though I found myself in an inconvenient and embarrassing situation, I could relax because I knew my business had a compelling story and predictable systems to keep things working.

The fact is that it's not difficult to be successful, you just have to follow a few principles and know who to go to for the right information.

For me, here is what these principles look like:

1. You need a great story around who you are and how you help people.

2. You need a system to tell that story in a way that gets results.

3. You need a great offer to present to your audience as a solution to their problems.

These principles won't keep your son from clogging your toilet, but they will give you the clarity and predictability you need to grow and succeed, no matter what challenges arise to meet you in your day.

These are skills I've mastered over 13 years of building my own businesses and coaching thousands of entrepreneurs with six-, seven-, and sometimes even eight-figure businesses. Once these principles are successfully applied, things get interesting. Much of the chaos and noise of marketing and sales is replaced with confidence and clarity. I've seen it repeatedly.

The Three Stories We Tell

There are three main stories people tend to tell in business. Each of these three stories can have a dramatic impact on your success. Though the same general storytelling tools can apply to all three, it's important to understand the differences in how and why we tell these stories.

The first is the story we tell ourselves, which is probably the most important. The story you tell yourself creates energy and meaning in what you do. It is the lens which helps you stay focused on your goals and get through the challenging times that are inherent in every successful entrepreneur's journey.

Second is the story you tell your audience. It's the conduit between you, your message, and the audience. If you go straight into the system, the end result, or the prescription without making it relevant, you'll be ignored. You need the context, meaning, and relevance, otherwise, you can't expect your audience to figure these things out for themselves; it's too direct, too raw. Without the story, you may not get the hookup or the engagement you need to help someone with the solution.

Many of us learn to take control of our own story the hard way. I changed the script on my life when my parents had a financial setback. My world changed. My inheritance just vaporized. Disappeared. It was like ripping up a winning lottery ticket and realizing, "This is actually up to me, and I'm not going to be gifted." I had to rewrite my script. I'm no longer a kid with a comfortable upbringing, living in a nice house in a lovely suburb of Sydney, going to an elite private school. Now I have to start from scratch, and I need a job. I was naïve until then. It was the biggest smackdown of all. Without a doubt, that's when I started changing my story by reprogramming the software in my head to take ownership of my life.

Finally, there's the story of your brand and why that's compelling to your team. I like to think my team and I are on a mission together, and it takes a good story to help them feel connected. Not only do we work for a company, we share a journey—this story of why we're doing what we do, and how we do it in my business. I want to enable them to have fantastic lives—it's one of my goals. It's not for them to just come to the workplace and pour on the coal for me every day. I want them to have a great life, and we can do this together as a collaboration. There are stories about why clients should talk to me, instead of my competitors, when they hear whispers of the kind of people I've been coaching, how my coaching has helped them achieve incredible results. It's very compelling.

Introducing Kyle Gray, Your Source For Story

You need to follow a few simple principles, and you need to know who to go to for the right information. Fortunately, if you're reading this book, you've already got that part figured out.

Kyle Gray came into my world through his efforts at WP Curve, a startup that was built around great storytelling and marketing. This is quite impressive for what you might think of as a "boring business" that provided WordPress development support. The founder, my friend Dan Norris, had announced he was looking for someone to help share that story and build awareness for the business. I know Dan pretty well; he's a brilliant writer and contrarian marketer. Kyle had some big shoes to fill stepping into this position.

The content WP Curve was creating was very compelling, and it was one of the few emails that made it through my filters each week. It went well beyond the general dry topics of a WordPress development firm. I kept seeing Kyle's name at the bottom of the articles, and I recognized his special abilities, because when I compare that to my business, I'm the one making the source content in my business, with my team curating it and organizing it. Dan had found someone who was able to do this stuff in his business so he could focus on bigger things. That's how I became aware of Kyle. I knew, of course, the downside was that Kyle would soon leave the business when he got strong enough, and sure enough, he did.

So what I saw was someone who had the natural ability and affinity for being able to convey a strong message in a super user-friendly way.

When you find anyone who's good at their thing, you see them rise through the initial phases of working for someone else to becoming independent and doing great collaborations, and then becoming the person you seek out as the source.

That's why I've invited Kyle to share his story and insights on my podcast several times, because I wanted to bring the source to my business. That's why I speak to Kyle about how to put together a compelling story structure. I'll seek his advice on how to compose it to get the point across in the most compelling way. He listens carefully and finds the story in my own experiences.

Kyle has the ability to help you tap into the source within you as well, even if you haven't recognized it yet.

Understanding the power of story and the different stories being told—to yourself, to your customers, to your team—is really a very important thing. Once you get the basics of what story actually is, which was covered in Kyle's book, *The Story Engine,* then comes learning how to apply the story and using it for great profit. It is a powerful weapon. In my whole time selling, marketing, and running a business, I know I've had some natural elements of it, but I didn't fully recognize its potential and how often it is literally the wrap-up that makes your product or service appealing to the customer. It's the conduit or connection, so it's really worth learning and maximizing it.

Which brings us back to the public restroom on the beach where I'm sitting on the toilet. Even though this is not my ideal way to start the day, I have to laugh at myself knowing that my story has been captured in a reliable system that's working for me. The system is a combination of tools, software, and team members that ensure my story is being told in a way that drives growth for my business. Many other business owners are going to have a worse day because they don't have their story captured in a process. We all need a great story, great lessons, great teaching, and a great offer to grow that business.

Better yet, these storytelling skills and this system eventually enabled me, thankfully, to have a far more luxurious abode just up the hill with multiple restrooms. The power of story really translates directly into lifestyle. I'll never have to repeat that day again.

Welcome to Selling With Story

In this book, Kyle lays out a simple framework to start crafting stories for your business and equips you with both powerful and practical tools to help you tell that story.

Since you're reading this book, it's likely that you already feel a need for storytelling in your business. Though for many practical-minded people out there storytelling may seem like a distraction from the bottom line, Kyle has designed this book to focus on frameworks and systems that will get you results.

If your goal is to build a memorable brand, stand out in a competitive marketplace, and sell more of your product or service, the frameworks in this book will help you do it.

Finally, what I love about this book and much of Kyle's other works is that the text on these pages is just the beginning. He's built many different templates, quizzes, and other great resources to help to put these ideas into action.

So, kudos to you for starting this process. I hope storytelling will help you transform your life and business like it did mine.

James Schramko,
Founder of SuperFastBusiness
and Author of *Work Less, Make More*.

INTRODUCTION
The One Clear Path to Sales

Storytelling saved my life. I never set out to be a storyteller. Looking back, it seems storytelling chose me.

It's graduation day. A day that should be one of the happiest of my life. I've just completed my master's degree. A proud day made even prouder by the fact I graduated debt-free and paid for it myself.

They call my name and I walk across the stage in front of my family and hundreds of others, my big gown masking a subtle limp. I make my best effort to bring a smile to my face, but it comes out a little crooked.

I'm here to celebrate the achievements of my mind, but I can't help but feel betrayed by my body. My jaw feels like it's about to fall off my face, I have to be careful with what I chew to avoid sparking nasty headaches, and I fear going to sleep at night and grinding my teeth. I fear starting my day each morning wondering if I am going to freak out with a spontaneous anxiety attack. I can't hike more than a quarter of a mile without some serious knee pain. As someone who loves being outdoors, this feels like a prison sentence. Somehow this does not feel like the basic "just getting older" or "overworked student" kind of stuff.

I remember one cold Monday morning when I almost couldn't get out of bed. Before I'm even fully awake, I'm already feeling stressed—already fearing the day. I'm staring at the constellations of speckled paint on my ceiling. My internal judge and jury have already come to their conclusion for why I'm feeling this way. It's obvious to me. I'm not a good entrepreneur, I'm not going to get what I want, I'm going to fail. This was the energy and mindset I would set myself against every day, and no matter how many Tony Robbins books I read, I could not seem to get past it.

Without realizing it, the story I was telling myself led to an unhealthy business. Working as a marketer for highly competitive coaches and startups, I needed every ounce of energy, creativity, and strategy I could muster. I was getting great results for these companies: I had helped a startup grow to seven figures in recurring revenue, helped transform other businesses with story, and I had written best-selling books. But I could not see past my own story. Which meant I charged less than I was worth, kept playing small, and missed out on big opportunities.

I started visiting various doctors, dentists, chiropractors, and other health professionals. I sank thousands and thousands of dollars into different treatments. Through various tests, I discovered I had a thyroid problem—the potential source of my suffering.

Over the next few years, I took thyroid supplements and other vitamins to manage things. I was feeling a little better, but I knew I was in a holding pattern. Was I just going to have to mask my symptoms for the rest of my life with a bowl full of pills every day?

I was still not clear on what exactly was happening to me, but in my research, I found over 80% of people who had thyroid issues like mine had something called "Hashimoto's."

Sure enough, I had it, too.

My first reaction to this was despair. "I've got an autoimmune disease . . . I'm stuck with this forever . . ." But I was tired of living this way, and I chose not to anymore. I decided to change my story. This diagnosis was not a condemnation, but a door opening. Now with some clarity on the problem I had, I could take steps to solve it.

What I didn't know at the time, is that Hashimoto's would be one of the best things to happen to me.

I began to read more and more about Hashimoto's and other similar chronic conditions. How do you get it? What does it feel like when you have it? How do you manage it? Digging through all kinds of books and other content trying to find an answer.

Until a twist of fate found me sitting across a lunch table from someone who would change my life forever.

"Hi, my name is Dr. Grace Liu, and I help people overcome autoimmune diseases through the gut."

My eyes widened as parts of my storytelling brain connected with everything I knew about health. I responded, "So your patients must feel like this and experience that—they feel like they have this problem, but it's really that," basically describing the last few years of my life.

She responded, "You need to come work for me." Dr. Grace was frustrated. She was brilliant at what she did, but her business was struggling to reach enough customers.

Dr. Grace and I worked out a deal where I would provide copywriting for her in exchange for her walking me through her Hashimoto's treatment. It didn't take long for each of us to add a lot of value to the other.

When she launched a new product or had a webinar to host, I helped her get clear on the real value in what she was offering and to cut out the medical speak that turns patients off. That boosted her sales. In turn, she guided me through my own healing process.

Within a month, the anxiety that once plagued me had cleared. After three months, I had never felt stronger, more confident, or clearer minded. With my biology working properly, there was less room for negative thoughts to creep in and weigh me down. I started making bigger leaps forward in my business. I had more energy in my work and outside of it.

With my new clarity, I realized the same work in storytelling I used to help consultants, coaches, and startups could make a big contribution to health and wellness. It could help thousands of people with conditions like mine recover their health and their lives.

With time, experimentation, and reflection, I developed a process that was simple enough for anyone to understand and implement. It makes it easy to communicate your value in a way that makes sense to your audience. I call it the "One Clear Path to Sales."

It's just three simple steps to communicate your value and sell more as a result:

1. **One Clear Message:** You must get clear on the exact message your customers need to hear to capture their attention and desire.

2. **One Clear Lesson:** Once you're clear on your message, you must craft amazing content that empowers, inspires, and educates your audience on how to get what they want. This builds their trust and desire to invest with you.

3. **One Clear Offer:** Finally, we must connect it with a key offer that aligns with their desire and your lesson.

The rest of this book is dedicated to these three steps and helping you create your own *One Clear Path to Sales*. You don't have to be a doctor or health-and-wellness entrepreneur to succeed with this process. But if it's simple enough for them, it's simple enough for you. Whether you're just getting started in your business and creating your first website, or you've been in the game a while, or you're a tech and business "guru," this process will help you reach more people, sell more of your product or service, and make your business work for you (not the other way around).

This process in this book is perfect for:

- Solopreneurs and personal brands looking for a fast yet scalable way to sell their products and services.

- Experts, consultants, coaches, and professionals who want to charge what they're worth and communicate their value with story.

- Entrepreneurs looking to create a scalable and reliable stream of income for their business.

- Marketing managers seeking to create powerful marketing campaigns.

This book goes beyond just storytelling. The real magic here happens when you can take your story and build it into a system that works for you. When you can capture your story in a system that carries people through the *One Clear Path to Sales* automatically, you free yourself from the trap of working "in your business." You'll know exactly what you need to do to create the revenues you desire.

None of the strategies in this book are new or cutting edge. They're time-tested approaches that have worked for decades (and in some cases, centuries). What *is* new are the tools and systems to apply these strategies to growing a business in the 21st century.

In Part I, we'll look at everything you need to do to get clear on what your audience wants, and how to connect their desires with your unique story in a way that creates a human connection.

In Part II, we'll explore how to create great teaching content to build desire for your products and services. Best of all, you don't need a lot of content to get the results you're looking for. We focus on the smallest amount of content you can create to get the most results. We'll also examine some strategies behind teaching in a way that makes people excited to work with you. By the time you present your offer to them, they'll be excited to hear it.

In Part III, we'll discuss making your offer. How you can entice your customers to move forward with you in a way that does not feel slimy or salesy. We'll also explore a few ways to scale up your offer and your marketing so you can turn it into an automated machine that works for you.

Throughout the book, I'll recommend many different tools and services you can use to help you on this journey. Many you can download for free at storyfunnel.co/resources.

Let's get started!

PART I

One Clear Message

Though your story is how your audience makes a personal connection with you, it's more about them than you. When you tell your story, your audience experiences it as if they are living it. So to craft a good story, we must first understand your audience, the message they want to hear, and how they experience their world.

Your Story Will Break Through the Noise

We live in a time of unprecedented opportunity. Technology has enabled us to connect with and serve people anywhere. It has created tools that have virtually no limit to how many people we can reach.

The problem is that it has empowered everyone. There's so much noise and competition for attention that you need something special to stand out. It's not enough to have the right knowledge or to be an expert in your field. There's virtually limitless information and knowledge available now.

Humans are not rational creatures. Strong emotions, not information, are what drive our decisions. When presented with "factual" information alone, only a small part of our brain responds.

This increased noise and flood of information have left your audience frustrated and craving something authentic: a human connection. A true connection with someone they can trust and relate to. That's what is truly rare and valuable these days, and nothing creates a true human connection better or faster than storytelling.

With a story, you can share what is brilliant and unique about you and build that connection with those you can help. Wrapping business concepts or ideas in a story can dramatically change how we process and interpret that same information.

Why It's Hard to Tell Our Own Story

Many startups, entrepreneurs, and small businesses struggle with defining their stories. It's difficult to communicate the value of what you do in a clear and concise way. When talking about our business or our work, we spout out a lot of insubstantial and technical details about what we do. As a result, we fail to connect with the people who could use our help the most.

Our story is ultimately what we're remembered for—it's the thoughts, feelings, and qualities that people associate with us—but most of us avoid putting in the work to understand and create our brand. You know, like we put off a trip to the dentist when we have a cavity.

Our story is something we create whether we're intentional about it or not. If we don't actively cultivate the story of our brand, we leave it up to others to create our story for us.

We're too close to the work we do to really see the value of it. We do what comes naturally to us and try to build a story around it later. This means we miss the true "gems" of who we are and what we do. In our marketing and sales conversations, these gems slip through the cracks, and our audience never truly gets to see why we've got the solution to their problems.

This results in us either underplaying everything we do or trying to share everything. Many of us are immersed in what we do every day; what others might see as genius, we overlook, thinking it's commonplace.

For others, it's easy to get caught up in the details of the work you do. Often we're tempted to be as specific and thorough as possible when describing what we do for people. Leaving out any detail can sometimes feel like deception, or like you're undercutting yourself. But you need to simplify your message so it's accessible for your customers.

Creating Your One Clear Message

In the first part of this book, we're going to overcome the challenges of telling your own story. You'll learn the tools to map and discover the stories that will serve your message and your business.

You'll be amazed at how simple your marketing and sales become once you have this clear message to work with. Having one clear message focuses your efforts and reduces the number of decisions you need to make. So you can stay focused on your brilliance instead of trying to figure out what the other person needs to hear.

Once you have your message and your story figured out, you can leverage it to grow your business in many different ways. Here are just a few:

- Webinars

- Public speaking

- Sales calls

- Podcast interviews

- Social media

- Sales videos

- The homepage of your website

- A concise and interesting response when someone asks you: "What do you do?"

The applications are virtually endless, and once you master the formulas and frameworks, you can continuously develop new stories and frameworks for your different products, audiences, ideas, and interests.

Get Ready For an Adventure

Discovering your story is a challenging process. It takes courage and an open mind to examine your values, your history, and your influences. You must be bold to be vulnerable and share the defining aspects of yourself.

I invite you to see this exploration as an adventure into who you are. Take this opportunity to examine yourself with fresh eyes and find the treasures buried within yourself.

CHAPTER 1

Before You Start Storytelling, You Need To Know Your Customer

There's one big mistake most people make when starting out in storytelling. They forget who the hero is. This is the first and most important secret to storytelling for your business.

You are not the hero, your customer is.

We must craft stories with your customer at the center. The story is *their* story, the conflict is what keeps them up at night, and the happy ending is how they define success. Our purpose in the story is just to set them on the path or to help them along the way.

Before we start storytelling, we need to get crystal clear on the world your customer (your hero) lives in. If you don't have a clear picture of their mind, fears, motivations, goals, and problems, you won't be able to serve them. Marketers use a tool called a *customer avatar* (also known as a buyer persona) to map out the mindset of their customers and guide their messaging.

In this chapter, I'll show you everything you need to develop your own customer avatar. I'm going to show you how to go deeper with your customer research and create an avatar system most entrepreneurs miss out on.

The Basic Ingredients of a Great Customer Avatar

There are some foundational pieces of information every customer avatar should include. These qualities help us picture a *real* person, not just a few bits of shallow demographic data.

With these basic ingredients, you can map out a powerful message that speaks right to the heart of your audience and inspires action.

Demographics

I mentioned earlier that demographics can only provide shallow insights into your audience. This is true when you only build an avatar around simple demographic data. Nevertheless, they're an important aspect of your avatar. Understanding demographics can shape your message and how you reach your audience.

Age - Knowing the age of your target market opens up many opportunities to relate to your audience. This sounds obvious, but most people don't fully leverage the storytelling power that comes from knowing someone's age. There are common trends, experiences, and attitudes within different generations.

The story you would tell about fitness and its value to a 20-year-old would be wildly different from what you would say to a 60-year-old. If you tried to sell the vision of six-pack abs glistening in the sun to a senior, your message would be ignored. Now consider what it would feel like to describe the benefits of longevity, quality of life, the ability to do more with their grandchildren, be more independent and take care of themselves, wake up with fewer aches and pains. That message would resonate.

Location - The location of your target customer can also greatly impact how you reach them and how you tell your story. What you would say to a native New Yorker would be different from someone from small-town Nebraska.

Marital Status - There are disparities between the mindsets of people who are single, married, or married with kids. This could impact their purchasing considerations, goals, and fears.

Someone without kids may be much more risk-tolerant and fully focused on their business, while someone with a family may be more conservative and want to make sure they have time to spend with their children.

Profession and Income - The language a doctor uses to describe his or her work, fears, and frustrations will be wildly different from that of a corporate real estate agent. Getting clear on the exact profession of your target customer can help you use language that is familiar to your audience. The more granular you can get on their profession, the more specific and powerful your language can be.

Their income can also give you insights into what kind of product you would create. If you're wanting to sell a $6,000 coaching package to teachers who only make $36,000 a year, then you're going to have more difficulty selling to them than to an executive making six figures.

Wants and Aspirations - What is the Core Desire You Speak to?

To capture and keep your audience's attention, you need to speak to a clear core desire. This is foundational for all your messaging. You need to speak to their desire in order to capture and keep their attention. This also helps you decide what kinds of products you should create for them.

The clearer and more specific you can get on their desires, the easier it will be to craft just the right story for them.

Keep in mind there's a big difference between external challenges and desires they face and the internal ones. For example: "I need new accounting software," or "I could really use a health coach." These are external *logical* problems—something that someone would type into Google in search of an answer. External desires are very important for identifying key storytelling points, teaching points, and developing features for your products.

But there's a deeper level to these desires which express themselves as internal, emotion-driven problems. Consider the same two examples mentioned in the last paragraph framed as an internal problem: "I want to get out of the office earlier so I can spend my time with my kids," or "I've tried everything, and I just can't seem to get rid of this brain fog or lose weight." Understanding the internal problems can really help you tell a story and write compelling copy that will have your audience wondering if you're reading their minds.

Think about it. You don't see any beer commercials advertising, "It will get you drunk" (except for a spoof ad for Samuel Jackson Lager by Dave Chappelle). They promise that as soon as you crack open a cold one, "You'll be the life of the party," or "You'll catch the attention of that beautiful woman on the beach."

A good way to bridge the external and internal desires of your audience is with a "so that" sentence:

"I want to fix [the problem you help them with] so that I'll finally be able to . . . [get what you really want]."

What do they really want? What are the good things they will experience with you?

- Save time at work so that you can spend time with your family.

- Save money at home so you can finally take that vacation.

- Delegate a "headache" task, so you can focus on your genius and grow your business.

Also consider higher-order thinking when considering what desires to speak to. This anticipates the effects that happen over the long term. When you take an action, there's usually an immediate result (first order), but then there are other consequences (or benefits) that happen later (second order).

Most of us only think of the first-order effects of our actions, but considering the downstream effects can help us tap into more and stronger desires.

Let's consider higher-order thinking for eating healthy for the first time:

First order (eating healthy for the first time) - This food tastes gross. I'm not feeling it, but I'll stick with it.

Second order (eating healthy for a week) - I'm feeling clearer and more energetic, and I figured out how to make kale not taste so gross when I cook it just right.

Third order (eating healthy for several months) - I've lost some weight, I feel amazing, and I finally have the confidence to ask for that promotion.

Think about the higher-order impacts of solving the problem you solve, and you may find new desires and wants to solve you didn't notice before.

Frustrations and Fears

These are the opposite emotions, but they are often tied in closely with wants and aspirations. They both drive action and attention in your customer's mind. People are much more loss-averse than they are willing to take risks and gain, meaning they'll do more to protect what they have.

What is your target audience afraid of losing or not getting? Is what they're holding on to helpful for them? Do you need to convince them to let go, or reassure them they won't lose what they're afraid to lose?

Are they afraid they will fail? What do they think will make them fail?

You also may need to consider these as obstacles or objections you need to overcome. Does working with you mean they'll need to give something up, maybe a strategy that works "well enough" or a lifestyle they're comfortable (but not happy) with?

Key Purchasing Considerations

If you can anticipate the key purchasing considerations, then you can build the evidence to support those considerations right into your stories and copywriting. You can stop common objections before your audience even realizes they have them.

Think of all the reasons someone would give for not wanting your product. Think of all the questions they would need to have answered to make your product or service a no-brainer for them.

Does your target customer need permission from someone else to make this purchase? Can you equip them with the tools they need to convince the person who controls the money?

Or can they buy it themselves?

What other tools, people, or services would your solution need to integrate or work with so they could use it easily?

Getting Clear on Your Ideal Customer's Mindset

One of the biggest mistakes people make when creating a customer avatar is to imagine them in a static situation. Demographics can only get us so far when we are trying to reach our customers. It gives us a good idea of where and how to target them, but it gives us an incomplete picture when deciding what story to tell them.

We also need to understand the current mindset of our audience. How much do they know about the problem you solve? Do they even know they have this problem? Is this something they're lightly researching, or is their hair on fire?

With clarity on the mindset of your perfect customer and the demographics, you can really hone your message, attract the right people, and feel comfortable turning away potential clients who may not be best served by you.

There are three basic stages in how someone's mindset evolves:

- **New -** This is someone totally new to the problem; they are learning the basics and probably have not tried much to solve it yet. New people may need convincing that they have a problem that needs to be solved.

- **Experienced -** This group knows they have the problem you solve; they have a basic understanding of the language around the problem and the pain it is causing them. They will need to see why they should work with you instead of doing it on their own.

- **Invested -** Someone who is invested has had this problem for a while; they've likely tried many solutions before. Invested people may need to be shown why you're different and better than all the other things they've already tried.

Mindset Example - Customer Success Software

Imagine you've got a startup that sells customer success software. You have a clear picture of your target audience demographics and a list of three prospects that fit the demographic profile perfectly.

New - Is in the early stages of a business but getting lots of customers. Things are growing fast, and new problems are emerging from that growth (that they're mostly ignoring). But they've never even heard of *customer success* before, much less feel like it's something they could use right now.

Experienced - Has been in business longer. They've got a basic understanding of *customer success* and have some half-baked systems implemented already. They know they've been churning customers faster than they would like and are researching some strategies to fix it.

Invested - Has been in business for a while, too. They have a huge customer base and know the value of customer success. They've even read a few books and done a few experiments. They know customer success is their top priority—essential for their sustainability.

Mindset Example - Health Coaching for Diabetes

New - This person has just barely been diagnosed with diabetes. They're probably feeling a lot of different emotions right now and are overwhelmed contemplating everything they need to do to manage this.

Experienced - This person has had their diagnosis for a few years; they know how to manage most aspects of diabetes but not others. Maybe they can't quite get control of their blood sugar or weight. They need someone to help with the specific aspects of diabetes they can't get control over.

Invested - This person has had diabetes for a while now. They've tried many different diets, exercises, and other treatments but never really seem to get control over their symptoms. They're looking for a different solution that will finally work for them.

With Clarity Comes Customers

Though they have the same core problem, each of the prospects listed in the example requires a different message to reach them. Each has a subtly different perspective that needs to be acknowledged and understood. Though any level of mindset can make for a great customer, it's best for your story to choose one and focus your message on them.

This level of clarity can also help you tailor your solution to fit the audience perfectly. You'll develop a better product that leaves them delighted. You'll also have a better framework to know which customers you can turn away. Some mindsets may not be as successful as others, and it's better for both of you if you're not wasting your time and resources with them.

So how can we anticipate this in our customer avatar?

Conclusion

Though your story is your own, your audience experiences it as if it were their own. So you need to build a story that resonates with their language, desires, fears, and understanding. The more your audience can see themselves and their desires fulfilled within your stories, the more successful you'll be in selling with a story.

I have a Customer Avatar Template I use in my business and with my clients to help map out the mind of my ideal customers. You can download it for free at resources.sellingwithstory.co.

Key Takeaways and Action Steps

- Demographics are an important foundation for under-standing your audience, but you must also understand their mindset.

- Explore how your audience experiences their problems on an external/practical level and an internal/emotional level.

- Think about the higher-order impacts of solving the problem you solve, and you may find new desires and wants to solve you didn't notice before.

- Some of your customers know a lot about the problem you solve; others don't even know they have it. You need to create messages to address these different levels of awareness.

CHAPTER 2

Grandma's Lasagna - Your Secret Recipe For Success

Let's go back to your childhood for a moment.

Was there a special meal that a special person would always make for you? Maybe it was your grandmother or some other comforting figure in your life. She made that special dish just for you when you came to visit. Maybe it was a delicious lasagna (but feel free to imagine whatever meal is special to you). Think of the smell of it cooking, the look of it on the plate in front of you, and of course, the delicious taste and texture as you eat it.

Absolutely delicious, right? But there was an unintended side effect to that amazing lasagna. Grandma has ruined lasagna for you for the rest of your life.

After eating Grandma's lasagna, all other lasagnas seem cheap and hollow. But how? She didn't use any "secret ingredients" to make hers so much better. It was your emotional connection to your grandmother that made her lasagna the only lasagna you're willing to eat.

I call this the *Grandma's Lasagna Effect.*

Wouldn't it be nice if your customers felt the same way about your product or service as you felt about Grandma's lasagna? That's what we're going to learn to do in this chapter.

A proprietary process is like Grandma's lasagna; it's your secret recipe for how you get results for your customer. It's a narrative for you to communicate the *what* and *how* behind the results you bring people.

Why Should You Have a Proprietary Process?

It Empowers You

The beauty of having a proprietary process is that it empowers you to talk about your business in a clear and thought-provoking way. This not only impacts how people receive your message but also how you deliver your message. With this process in place, you draw upon your own story and the deep aspects of who you are. This creates something bigger than yourself and changes how you show up every day.

You'll Get More Clients

The magic of a good proprietary process is it gives your prospects a way to visualize being successful with you. It creates a road map to working with you; they have every step outlined for them and understand how each step will serve their goals. Instead of being bogged down in technical details, they're imagining themselves experiencing the success and satisfaction of working with you.

Since they have a complete and clear view of what working with you will look like, and how you'll get results for them, they're much more likely to trust you and work with you.

You Can Charge Higher Prices

The *Grandma's Lasagna Effect* you create with your process transforms your business from another "me too" among hundreds of competitors to the one and only business that provides what you offer. You become an instant authority on your own product, and people trust experts and those who know something well.

This means you don't have to compete on price anymore. No longer do you need to discount yourself when your client mentions "I just talked to Jimmy down the street and they said they could do it for half." Nobody wins in the race to the bottom.

You can finally charge what you're worth because you have a tool to explain the unique value and experience you bring to the world, and that there's nowhere else they can get it.

It Makes Presenting Easier and More Effective

Let's face it, when most of us talk about our businesses, we might as well be speaking German (unless of course, your native language is German). Usually, reaching the point where we feel like we've actually explained what we do requires several minutes of dull details that leave our listener wishing they never asked.

Whether you're speaking to someone you met at an event, on stage at the same event, or on a sales call, your proprietary process gives you a tool to talk about what you do in a way that gets people to lean in instead of tune out.

You'll Have a Better Team

A process changes how you interact with customers and your audience, but also how you work with your internal teams.

Your process makes the unique value you provide clear and gives more context to your team to see how they fit into that story. When they understand your process and a bigger picture of what your vision is, they grow a deeper sense of purpose in their work. They're not just doing a job, they're changing the world.

It's also likely that your *why* behind the process, or who you serve with that process, will resonate with them. This creates added meaning for them in their work, which leads to more motivation, productivity, and loyalty. A meaningful job that connects with their own *why* means it will be much more difficult for your competitors to try to poach your talent even if they offer higher pay.

Example Processes

Podcast Launch Gameplan By FullCast

THE ULTIMATE PODCAST LAUNCH GAMEPLAN™

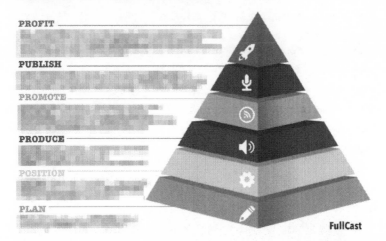

The Ultimate Podcast Launch Gameplan™ is FullCast's strategy for launching a successful podcast.

Launching a podcast can be overwhelming for many people, which either results in:

- A launch that does not get results

- No launch at all and burnout

This process simplifies a podcast launch and makes it step-by-step instead of a chaotic sprint. Fullcast uses this process as a high-value lead magnet they offer for free, but it is also their process for a service they offer to their clients. Those who start with the lead magnet get educated and invested in the process, and if they choose to work with FullCast, they'll already understand what's going to happen. This means their sales process is easier.

One Clear Path by Kyle Gray

This is a process we've already started to explore, but I want you to be aware of this while reading the rest of this book. Thus, this entire book can be an example of a strong process. I use this same process in webinars, presentations, and to develop a marketing strategy for my clients.

The One Clear Path to Sales - A Faster Way to Sell with Storytelling

One Clear Message - We get clear on the exact message your customers need to hear to capture their attention and desire.

One Clear Lesson - We craft amazing content that empowers, inspires, and educates your audience on your unique process. This builds trust and desire to invest with you.

One Clear Offer - We connect it with a key offer that gets results for your customers and growth for your business.

Many people overcomplicate the process of selling a product or service online. They often try to add a lot of extra bells and whistles, such as:

- Long books

- Teaching too much on webinars

- Telling distracting stories that don't add value

By following the *One Clear Path to Sales* process, entrepreneurs get results faster for their business by creating an easy and automated system that sells for them.

The Namaste of Sales by Amira Alvarez

Amira Alvarez helps empower women entrepreneurs to increase their income through better sales. Her process, *The Namaste of Sales,* reframes sales from pushy to authentic and high integrity. This enables her audience to sell more and charge what they're worth while still feeling aligned with their purpose.

Building Your Proprietary Process

Start With Specific Results for the Customer

Most of us focus on what we do, with the specific nuts and bolts of how that will work. Your proprietary process focuses on results and what your customer will get out of the process. By focusing on results, you instill confidence in your listener, and they will begin to imagine themselves experiencing the results and benefits you offer.

Starting out, your process and promise should be easily explained in one sentence that goes something like this:

"We do [name of your process], so you can [solve a problem] and get [what you really want]."

Each section should have a clear result that you can promise at the end.

Build a Success Path - What Does it Take to Get Them There?

Once you're clear on the big result you get, you need to create a road map for how you'll get them there. This is known as a *success path*. A success path makes it easy for people to see what it will take to get the results they want and helps them put what you teach into context wherever they are on that path. A success path is crucial because it removes a lot of uncertainty in working with you. They know where they're going and what comes next.

This means creating three to five steps or ingredients to your process. Keeping the number of steps to three is recommended because it's easy for people to remember and internalize, but there's plenty of processes out there with many more steps.

Steps - Your process goes in a sequence, each step builds on the previous step, leading to the ultimate result you promise.

Ingredients - These do not need to be completed in a sequence. Instead, focus on getting the right balance and mastery over each of the ingredients and then combining them to lead to the result you want.

Building steps into your process allow your customers to see a big-picture view of how you'll get the results for them, and it allows them to have more context and meaning for each step in the process.

It can be difficult to decide how many steps—or which steps—to include in your process. Below is a simple framework for a three-step process you can use to ensure you have an engaging method that gets results.

Step 1 - Onboarding/Discovery: Your first step should involve collecting information from your customer or audience. This can take the form of an assessment or discovery call, getting people on the phone, and mapping out a strategy for them can be very powerful.

Assessments or quizzes also make for very good lead magnets, collecting new leads and gathering information on your audience while providing personalized value to your prospects. We'll talk about that more in a later chapter.

Step 2 - Build: You take the information you collected in your assessment and start to build a tool or plan based on that information.

Step 3 - Action: With the new tool or plan built, your customer now has what they need to get the result they desire if they take the action necessary to get it.

Connect Each Step of Your Process to Your Story (or Use a Metaphor)

A proprietary process is a scaffolding for your stories. It gives you predictable and relevant opportunities to share your personal stories while discussing your process.

You'll want a story to connect with the big picture of the process. Usually, this is your origin story. How did you discover this process? How were you the first case study that proved the power of the process? What was the pain you experienced that motivated you to take action and solve the problem for yourself?

You'll also want to have some smaller stories ready to help illustrate every individual step of your process.

Your Process Should Have Something For Everyone

Your process should have information and stories that someone at any level of awareness could get value from. If you only address topics and ideas that beginners can understand, then the experts will feel your service is not for them. You can solve this problem by ensuring you use stories that address every segment of your audience.

Within each step of your process, you should outline concrete actions that people can take to get the result you promise. Within these steps, you need to have something for your whole audience. Remember your audience has a mix of experience and familiarity with what you're teaching. You need to reach both the beginners and the experts in your presentations.

When designing your steps, make sure you address:

Beginners - Something that someone who is totally new to your concepts can take action on right away.

Experts - Something to show the experienced professionals in the audience that you're not just repeating what everyone else is saying.

Short-term Wins - Something that can get fast results and be applied immediately to their business.

Long-term Wins - Something that takes time and investment, but yields good long-term results.

Embedding Sales Into Your Stories

When people know they're being pitched, sometimes their defenses go up, or they check out. Often, when speaking on stages, webinars, or podcasts, we won't be allowed to directly pitch our products, anyway.

But there's a way to use stories to communicate how your audience can move forward with you without putting their guards up.

The parts of the brain that process sales are different from the ones that process content. With sales, they're naturally skeptical and distrusting. With content, they're open and perceive it as valuable.

Often in webinars, podcast interviews, or other content, we make a very visible transition from education to selling, which feels awkward and forced.

If we embed stories into our process—stories about taking the next steps to move forward in working with us, others who have done it, and what it involved—we can educate our audience on our product suite without triggering their defenses.

Here are a few ways to embed the next steps into your content:

- **Testimonies** - Instead of just pasting a quote, tell a story of how a client used your process to get results.

- **Next Steps** - Right before you're about to teach something powerful, tell a little story about how, with your clients, you do X. Or mention how this is one of the favorite strategies people in your membership site use.

- **Value Offer** - If you give away a gift or lead magnet at the end of your content, or in a podcast interview, mention it early on in your teaching. Just talk about why it's useful or how people use it, build desire and perceived value so they anticipate the gift and understand its value to them.

Embedding Case Studies

One of the most powerful and compelling stories you can tell is one of a successful client who has overcome the exact challenge or objection that your audience is feeling. You should have stories ready for each section of your process. This helps them envision success in their own future and builds their desire to work with you.

When trying to think of case studies, most people only think of the stories where someone has gone through your full process and succeeded. While this is one good story to have ready, it may not be relatable for everyone.

Here are a few different types of case study stories to build around your process:

1. **The First Step** - Tell a story about how a client succeeded in taking his or her first step in your process. This is perfect to get people off the fence.

2. **Beating "The Dip"** - Seth Godin's book, *The Dip,* talks about how most projects or endeavors you start usually get some early momentum but experience a dip before they become really successful. How and when will your audience experience "The Dip" in your process? Create stories about your clients who have overcome "The Dip."

3. **The Full Journey -** You also want to have stories from clients who have gone through the whole process and experienced the rewards at the end. These poster-child case studies are a big testament to your process.

4. **Possibility -** Perhaps you don't have case studies yet because it's a new product or you're new to your industry. In this case, look for people who have achieved a similar goal to what you outline in your process. Just make sure to be clear that you're just exploring possibilities, not taking credit for success you didn't help create.

Embedding is Like "Salt" in a Cake

More food references . . . Hopefully, you're not reading this while hungry.

When baking a cake, you need to throw in a pinch of salt or it does not taste quite right; but if you add too much, it ruins the cake. Embedding works in a similar way. You should embed stories about your offers very lightly throughout your content and focus primarily on high-value education and adding value to them. Only lightly mention your products or working with clients in your stories and spend most of your time in the teaching. This will be enough to plant the seed of desire for your products or services without triggering their sales alarms.

Conclusion - Start With One

I recommend you start with just one—create a process that describes the full spectrum of your business and the results the customer can expect. This will become the foundation for your marketing and brand storytelling.

Once you have your foundational process established, you can create multiple proprietary processes in your business.

As you begin to create multiple processes, think about the "big picture" result you want to achieve for people, and try to create a proprietary process to solve the major problems that are keeping your audience from that result. Your processes should relate to each other, but they should not overlap too much. Otherwise, you'll confuse your customers and muddle your messaging.

I've created a simple Process Building Template to help you create and refine your own proprietary process. You can download it at resources.sellingwithstory.co

Key Takeaways and Action Steps

- A proprietary process is an easy way to use storytelling to differentiate yourself in a crowded market.

- Keep your process to three to five simple steps and build a story or metaphor around those steps. The steps should lead to a key result your audience wants.

- Make sure when teaching your process that you add value to both beginners and experts, and both short- and long-term strategies.

- You can talk about your products and services while teaching by mentioning them as stories to reinforce your teaching points.

CHAPTER 3

Simple Frameworks For Better Storytelling

A blank page can be intimidating when trying to craft your own story. Frameworks and mental models are excellent tools for problems like this. They help us take new perspectives and new paths of thought which help us escape from the common mental ruts we find ourselves in.

There are two frameworks well suited to help us understand our story and tell it to our audience in a way that resonates with them: the *Hero's Journey* and the *Buyer's Journey;* each has certain strengths and weaknesses which we'll examine.

The Hero's Journey

The Hero's Journey is the model for popular stories throughout history. Though its roots go back to early mythology, it wasn't until the 20th century that Joseph Campbell noticed the pattern in these ancient myths and stories and coined the term "Hero's Journey" (thus creating his own proprietary process for storytelling). This model is so effective because it mirrors how we process our own stories, conflicts, and experiences.

You can see the Hero's Journey play out in your favorite movies, plays, and TV shows, as well as talks, webinars, and sales letters. The Hero's Journey has all the elements of a story that we as humans can't help but become immersed in:

- **Conflict and Uncertainty** - Conflict, and the tension it brings, are the key elements that keep us hooked.

- **Risk and Reward -** What good is an adventure without some treasure to find?

- **Transformation** - The adventure is a process of transformation—a process we all undergo regularly in our own lives.

The Hero's Journey is divided up into 12 stages. But in my experience, you don't need to understand the details of all 12 stages to make the most of this framework. I've broken those 12 stages down into four acts which are easier to grasp.

Act 1 - Status Quo, Call to Adventure, and Assistance

The beginning of the hero's story. Everything is normal in the world, but there's a sense of dissatisfaction. There's a problem holding the hero back, or life is just not as good as it could be.

There's a desire or an invitation for something more—something better. This could also be a problem that is bothering the hero, and it forces him out of his comfort zone. This desire or problem should resonate with your audience and what they desire as well.

The hero gets some help or guidance to help set her on her path. This could be a mentor giving her guidance on what to do next or giving her a tool that will help her on her journey.

Act 2 - Departure, Trials, and the Approach

The hero leaves the comfort of the familiar world to set off on a new adventure. He gets some early wins and a boost of confidence, maybe even a little hubris.

This is where the struggle begins. The thrill of those early wins has vanished, and it's not so easy anymore. The hero hits some unexpected setbacks.

Things are getting harder. The hero is losing momentum and experiencing doubts. The big monster she must confront is on the horizon. The hero is experiencing the fears your audience wants to avoid.

Act 3 - Crisis, Treasure, and the Result

Just when you thought it couldn't get any worse . . . it does. The hero hits rock bottom. He experiences painful emotions and starts thinking about the long-term consequences and ramifications of not solving this problem. The hero is about to give up . . .

Until . . .

The hero finds the thing that can turn it all around. Maybe it's an idea, a tool, a new way of looking at things, a new person or a process.

The hero takes action, using this newfound treasure to solve the big problem she is experiencing. The rewards and results the hero has been hoping for since the beginning of her journey are finally within reach.

Act 4 - Return, New Life, Resolution

The hero returns to the ordinary world stronger and wiser than before. Sometimes the world isn't so ordinary anymore; it's new and upgraded. He reflects on the long road it's been to get here and is grateful for the adventure. With his new knowledge/treasure, he can serve those he returns to in new ways and bring new wealth to his home.

With a new perspective and new life, the hero sees new options and opportunities. By overcoming a big challenge, new doors open up that she didn't notice before.

Free from the challenges and fears that once threatened him, the hero is now free to live the life he wanted. Now he must figure out how to share this new wisdom with the rest of the world.

Visualizing the Hero's Journey

Trying to keep all 12 stages together on paper like this can be challenging, but in many cases, you can map out the Hero's Journey on a graph. This makes it much easier to work with and understand; plus, you'll be happy to see most good stories follow a predictable path. The vertical and horizontal axes represent good (or bad) fortune and time. Here's how the Cinderella story looks as a graph.

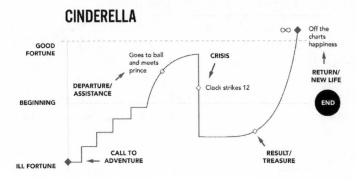

Let's take a look at another classic story that recently returned to the big screen: *The Hobbit*. This is a classic tale of an unsuspecting character who's just looking to live a modest and quiet life. He gets visited by a wizard and sets off on an adventure that will change his life forever. Take a look at the visualization of Bilbo Baggins' journey there and back again and see how it fits in with the Hero's Journey.

(Feel free to skip the visual below if you have not read/seen it and don't want any spoilers.)

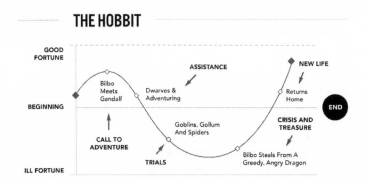

Okay, let's do one more, a little more practical one. I could make graphs of my favorite movies and books all day. But let's look at it in the context of a presentation. One of the most popular TED Talks of all time: Brené Brown's, The Power Of Vulnerability.

Grab your phone or computer and search "The Power Of Vulnerability," and this 10-minute talk will appear. Watch the talk and compare it with the chart below. Try to be aware of the feelings and ideas you're experiencing as she shares her own story.

Brené is an expert storyteller and weaves stories into her writing, speaking, and conversation effortlessly. The great thing about this talk is how well she weaves in her key teaching points with her own story of discovering what she is teaching, her own struggles with being vulnerable, and how she applied what she learned from her research to her own life.

The Benefits and Weaknesses of the Hero's Journey

This framework is so powerful and effective because we as humans are wired for storytelling. Our powerful imagination not only follows stories but puts ourselves in the shoes of the hero—their problems, ideas, and goals become ours. This is why you start screaming at the television when your favorite character is about to make a bad decision.

While the Hero's Journey is excellent at helping to create an emotional and relatable experience for our customers, it does little to illustrate the logic of a buying decision. Without addressing the crucial questions your audience has before making a purchase, you'll inspire good feelings but no action.

Another challenge with the Hero's Journey is the complexity. It is difficult to memorize and keep all the different stages straight. For a dedicated writer looking to create the next classic novel or movie, it's a great tool. But for the entrepreneur just beginning the path of storytelling, it can be overwhelming.

Not to worry, though. In the next chapter, I have a simplified storytelling framework I want to share with you. But first, we need to explore another journey into the mind of a buyer trying to make a decision.

The Buyer's Journey

In Chapter 1, we introduced the *Buyer's Journey* as a way to visualize the decision-making process a customer goes through to make a purchase. This journey has four phases: Know, Like, Trust, and Delight.

Each phase requires you to overcome a certain set of challenges or obstacles in your buyer's mind to persuade him or her to move forward. You can create content that is optimized to target each of these goals instead of trying to create something that does them all. This helps us hone in on exactly what to create.

Know

Your customer needs to be aware you exist and what problem you solve.

At this stage, people probably aren't even sure if the problem you solve is the most important one for them to work on right now. They probably have many options to choose from. This phase likely makes up about 80% of your audience, most are just looking for information, and are likely to buy in 12-plus months.

Like

They need to know why you're different from everyone else who solves this problem.

You want to present yourself as someone who can solve this problem and as a brand that resonates with your ideal customer. This phase will make up around 17% of your audience. People who are in this stage are comparing different products or services and are likely to buy in the next 30–90 days.

Trust

They need to know you're a good fit for the problem they have, and that you can deliver the result they want.

At this point, you've proven yourself to be competent and likable to your audience, so from here, you must convince them you are a good fit for them and that working with you will be a good investment of their time, energy, and money. This phase is by far the smallest segment of your audience, probably just 3%, but it's also the most valuable segment because they're ready to buy right now.

At this stage, you start to eliminate the buyer-and-seller dynamic between you and your customer and replace it with *a subject matter expert* and *interested party*. The members of your audience are more willing to share information about their businesses with you at this stage.

Also, remember that trust does not stop after the sale—you must consistently maintain and build on the trust you develop with those in your audience even after they've become your customers. To do so, create things that will help your current customers be more successful as well as remind them how much value you add to their lives.

Delight

The journey does not stop at the purchase; your customers need to be reminded of the value you add for them even after the purchase. It's not something that comes naturally to most. Many people in the modern world are so future-oriented they rarely take the time to celebrate their achievements. They climb one mountain and immediately begin looking for the next peak before they even enjoy the view.

Remind them of the progress they've made working with you, delight them by celebrating this progress with them. This inspires loyalty, future purchases, and advocacy for your business.

The Buyer's Journey is a powerful way to map out and plan marketing campaigns, sales funnels, and content. But . . . if we only target the "logical" side of the brain of our audience, then our message will fall flat. We won't create that emotional connection and drive to get people to take action.

Conclusion

Both of these journeys are powerful mental frameworks, but only when they're combined do they tell the story of our business in a meaningful way that drives growth.

The interesting part about these frameworks is they outline different perspectives of the same process. The Hero's Journey maps out how your customer is experiencing and engaging with your brand, while the Buyer's Journey maps out the logical decision-making process which happens in tandem with the experience. By using them both together we can outline a storyline that emotionally engages our audience and provides them with everything they need to make a buying decision.

Key Takeaways

- Use storytelling frameworks to make it easier to get your story ideas out of your head and onto a page.

- The Hero's Journey is the most common storytelling framework. You don't need to use every stage to tell a great story.

- The Buyer's Journey is powerful for helping to understand the mindset of your audience and what they need to make a decision to buy from you.

CHAPTER 4

The Crossroads of the Hero's Journey and the Buyer's Journey

By combining the experience of the Hero's Journey with the decision points of the Buyer's Journey, we get a checklist that helps us better tell the story of our brand and naturally resonates with our ideal customers. Since it's the crossing of two different journeys, I call this the *Crossroads Formula*. It also has four stages:

- **The Call** - Building awareness of the problem.

- **The Quest** - Sharing your unique approach to solving the problem.

- **The Leap** - Building trust and emotion with your audience to get them to take action.

- **The Return** - Reflecting on the better life you can provide your audience with your solution.

The Crossroads Formula takes the stages of the Buyer's Journey and then matches those to the different stages of the Hero's Journey. This allows you to both inspire the mind and the heart within the story. It connects key emotions and decisions in a way that inspires action with your audience.

Let's examine the different stages of the Crossroads, and look at some prompt questions to help inspire stories for you to tell for each stage.

The Call - Building Awareness

As mentioned in the previous chapter, the "Know" phase of the Buyer's Journey is all about building awareness. Your goal during this phase is simply to capture the attention of your audience. You don't need to try to sell anything; they just need to start identifying with the story you're telling.

Using the Call in Stories

The beginning of the hero's story. Everything is normal in the world, but there's a sense of dissatisfaction. There's a problem holding the hero back, or life is just not as good as it could be.

There's a desire or an invitation for something more, something better. This desire usually comes from a problem. People very rarely decide to do anything worthwhile on their own; they're forced on the path from something outside them.

This could also be a problem that is bothering the hero, and it forces him out of his comfort zone. This desire or problem should resonate with your audience and what they desire as well.

Along with a problem, the hero also encounters a guide. This could be a mentor giving her guidance on what to do next or a tool that will help her on her journey. This is your role in the story. You're the guide to the hero who sets your audience on the journey to achieve big goals and overcome challenges.

Here are some prompt questions to help you come up with some stories for *the Call:*

1. Describe a time when you realized you had a need to solve the same problem your audience is currently facing.

2. Talk about a time when you thought everything was fine, but you were surprised by a problem you weren't prepared for.

3. Describe a time when you were struggling, then a change in your mindset or the way you were looking at the problem brought success to you.

The Buyer's Mindset in the Call

The purpose of *the Call* in your story is to create interest. Your audience needs to have a reason to keep listening. Your listeners are silently asking themselves, "Is this a story I want to listen to?" or "Is this a problem I want to solve?"

To get those in your audience to join you on this adventure, they need to know why they should care about this problem.

You can start by outlining the surface level problem:

- Not enough sales

- Symptoms of poor health like fatigue, belly fat, or brain fog

- The old car keeps breaking down

Calling out the problem here is enough to get their attention, but to get them to really engage, you need to go deeper and describe the

implications of this problem. Why is this a problem? What will happen
if this problem goes unaddressed?

- If I don't sell enough, I'm going to have to close the business,
  get a job, or be unable to provide for my family.

- I don't feel like myself anymore, I used to have all this
  energy, and now I can't be bothered to do the things I once
  loved.

- What if this old junker car breaks down in the middle of a
  road trip? Am I wasting money maintaining this thing?

Go deeper with your stories and always use the language your
audience uses when describing the problem. The feeling of conflict
and pain in a story gets your listeners invested in the journey and
identifying with the hero.

The members of your audience will not only be wondering if the
problem you're describing is one they want to solve, but why you care
about solving it and why you're someone who's worth listening to.
How have you walked in their shoes before? They need to know
you've experienced the pain they feel. They need to know you have
the key to the problem. You've found the shortcut and can show them
the way. How can your experience and perspective help them solve
this problem?

The Quest - Differentiation from the Competition

Congratulations! You successfully have your audience's rapt attention!
But you're still walking on a tightrope to keep it. You've begun to tap
into the problem this audience has, but there's currently nothing
separating you from the hundreds of others who offer the same

solution. In this phase, you will begin to present what makes you different, and the unique benefits to your approach.

At this point, the people you speak to may be willing to share their contact information with you or even make a small purchase with the right motivation.

Using "The Quest" in Stories

The hero leaves the comfort of the familiar world to set off on a new adventure. She has some early wins and a boost of confidence, maybe even a little hubris. The road seems easy at the beginning of the journey, but soon after her early victories, she realizes the quest may be more challenging than she realized.

This is also where the hero experiences a major failure or comes up against a problem they can't solve. They're ready to give up. The failure or challenge in the story is the same problem keeping your audience from the result they want to see in their own lives.

Here are some prompt questions to help you come up with some stories for *the Quest:*

1. When did you make a decision not to do something, and then later found out that your decision had a high cost?

2. Describe a time when you had to learn an important lesson the hard way.

3. Describe a time when you hit rock bottom and how that forced you to change your perspective on a problem.

The Buyer's Mindset in the Quest

Like the hero, your listeners could use a quick win in your story. A quick win can also be clarity in how to solve the problem. This is the point in your story where you may want to start giving specific teaching points for your audience to accent your story. The education and presentation in this part of your story help to show why you're different from your competition and should help to draw in those who resonate with your unique approach.

There's magic in getting a quick win for your audience. It begins to set you apart as someone who really knows how to get things done and is not just selling "snake oil." It also helps instill some trust that those in the audience really can get what they want. Consider that deep down they may not yet believe they can be successful in solving this problem. By giving them a little bit of information or a strategy so they can experience a quick win, they start to see the potential of success, and the light at the end of the tunnel.

Your audience members may be dragging their heels because they don't know how they can solve their problem. This is where your *Grandma's Lasagna*, as discussed in an earlier chapter, can really serve as a road map for their success.

After your quick win, your customers are excited to move forward and go deeper with you. But just because they have a road map to success or a picture of what life will be like when they succeed, does not mean they're there.

The challenge in *the Quest* is to simultaneously instill confidence in your audience. You want to assure people they can achieve their goals and overcome these challenges, but also stretch the gap between where they are and what it will take to get them what they want.

They're weighing whether it's worth the effort and investment, so show them what's at stake if they don't take action. Why can't they ignore this problem? How will it get worse? How will it keep them from getting what they want?

Through your storytelling, and possibly some of their experience, they start to realize how much work and effort must go into getting what they want. Their growing desire will keep them enthralled to learn more about your Grandma's Lasagna to get the results they deserve.

Instead of trying to frame yourself as the key to their problems, focus on your process. With your Grandma's Lasagna, they can be successful and overcome the challenges on their path. This enables you to talk about your solution and the results your audience can experience without coming off as too salesy or self-promoting.

The Leap

The Leap is the crucial decision point in the story. The hero, now at his lowest and most vulnerable point, must choose whether to give in to the challenge before him, or take courage and face it. This is the leap of faith that transforms the hero and helps him find the true solution to his problem.

This mirrors your audience's decision whether to move forward with you. People need to trust you enough to make their own leap of faith and invest in you. You demonstrate why you are trustworthy here by showing you also struggled in your journey and understand what your audience is feeling.

Using "The Leap" in Stories

The hero, though at the lowest point in her journey, summons the courage to give it one more try. But she has learned from her mistakes and the shortcomings that once held her back.

With a fresh perspective, the hero finds the thing that can turn it all around. Maybe it's an idea, maybe it's a tool, a new way of looking at things, a new person or a process.

But the solution is not so easily handed over. It takes a leap of faith to make it work: making an investment, facing a fear, taking a risk. He faces a key choice here, to take the leap and change his life, or continue on his own.

The hero takes action and uses this newfound treasure to solve the big problem she is experiencing. The rewards and results the hero has been hoping for since the beginning of her journey are finally within reach.

Here are some prompt questions to help you come up with some stories for *the Leap:*

1. Describe a time when you were stuck, and a mentor helped get you unstuck and moving forward.

2. Describe a time when you were struggling, then a change in your mindset or the way you were looking at the problem brought success to you.

3. When is a time you've experienced joy and satisfaction after achieving a goal you've worked on for a long time?

The Buyer's Mindset in the Leap

At this point, people are looking for solutions. Here is where you can present your product or service as the key to overcoming this challenge.

You want to illustrate how your solution has helped more people than just yourself. This is an excellent place in a story to share testimonials and case studies of people you have worked with before. Show them being successful with your process and focus on them as the heros, avoid crediting yourself with their success.

In order to trust you enough to make their own leap, people need to know what kind of results they are going to get from it. Help them understand (in specific numbers, if possible) what they can expect to get from overcoming this challenge.

The Return

The hero's return is relatively short compared to the other areas as far as how much time you spend telling this part of the story. You've reached the point of resolution and now must close your story, leaving your audience with warm emotions and inspiration.

Using "The Return" in Stories

The hero returns to their ordinary world stronger and wiser than before. She reflects on the long road she has taken to get here and is grateful for the adventure. She realizes she is stronger, smarter, and kinder now. The things which used to bother or challenge her no longer seem so threatening.

With a new perspective and new life, the hero sees new options and opportunities. With the big challenge overcome, new doors open up he didn't notice before. Now he must figure out how to share the wisdom he has gained with the rest of the world.

- Describe a time when learning an important lesson or making an investment opened up new opportunities for you to live the life you wanted to live.

- Describe a goal or thing you always wanted to achieve or have but thought was out of your reach until you made a key change.

- Share stories of how your clients, with your process, are living better lives because of overcoming this challenge.

The Buyer's Mindset in the Return

At this point, someone has made the choice to become a customer and purchase from you or may have already bought a product. It's here that you want them imagining how their life is going to be better.

To close your story well there needs to be a call to action. You want to challenge your audience to be better. But you also want to understand there are two kinds of people listening to your story. There are the tactically oriented people who are looking for something practical, and there are emotionally oriented people looking for a feeling.

Knowing this, it's best to challenge both with two separate calls to action.

One that encourages them to download something or make a change in their businesses. Here are a few examples of calls to action you could use:

- Download this cheat sheet which will help you find the problems areas in your SEO.

- Try this breathing exercise every morning for a week and see how you feel.

- Please book a strategy call with me to build a plan on how you can get . . .

The second should be an emotional call to action, something that pulls on the heart strings of your audience.

- There's someone close to you that you have not yet forgiven.

- Take a moment to remind someone close to you how much you love them.

- The next time you see someone in need . . .

Your audience has become a customer and is happy with what they purchased. What opportunities can you present them to go deeper with you and get more of the good results you provide? Do you have upsells, other products, or loyalty programs?

Applying the Crossroads to Your Marketing and Sales

Though we'll discuss the details for different marketing tools and strategies you can use in later chapters of the book, you'll also want to understand how to apply this framework to those tools. Here are two simple ways you can use the Crossroads in your marketing to make it easy to tell better stories and get better results.

Tell a Full Story - Opening Stories for Your Talks / Webinars / Podcasts / Etc.

The Crossroads is a perfect template for an opening story for any presentation. Use the full four steps to create a story that has the highs and lows of an adventure and shows why you are passionate about the topic.

Even when telling a full story, consider that it does not have to be just one single story. You can weave together a bunch of vivid moments from your own journey and experience with your clients to create a Crossroads story of your own.

Tell a Short Story - in Your Email Automations, Sales Videos, and Social Media

Sometimes you don't need to tell a full story to get the point across. You won't always have the opportunity to move your audience through the full story in one sitting, particularly if you're marketing online through content, social media, and emails.

Here's a story you could use to tell for *the Call* and show the cost of inaction:

"I felt stressed and overwhelmed in my business. My business coach kept telling me it was time to hire some help. I kept resisting the idea because I had some doubts about hiring. The tasks and stress kept piling up, but I was not making any meaningful progress. Finally, after a year, I brought on an assistant, and my world changed. I was able to focus on the work of growing my business and handed off many of the time-consuming repetitive tasks in my business. The following year my business more than doubled, and I realized how much money I had left on the table by not hiring sooner."

Here's another example you could use for a story in *the Quest* stage:

"When I first started investing in real estate, I dived in feet first. I had owned a home for a long time, so I figured I could handle investing in a few more. At the time I had no idea the real challenges in real-estate investing are managing all the people. Tenants moving out without warning. Managing relationships of everyone in the triplex. I knew I was really in over my head when one nasty tenant decided to flood the basement after refusing to pay rent."

You don't need more than a few lines to tell a compelling story that hits the emotional and rational areas of the mind.

Now, consider how little stories like this could fit in with the many different marketing assets, like email automation, sales videos, and social media. Or to reinforce specific teaching points in a talk or webinar. We're going to talk about more marketing tools like email automation in the next section of the book. So don't fret if you're unfamiliar with that term.

Instead of trying to cram a whole story into every piece of content you create, think about where in the Buyer's Journey your audience is at the time. You can use the individual pieces of the Crossroads Formula to create short but powerful stories that answer the questions your audience is asking.

If it's in the early "Know" stages, maybe you tell one which focuses on *the Call* to build interest in the problem you solve and give them some information that will give them a quick win.

If you're later in the "Trust" stages of the Buyer's Journey, like in a follow-up email after a webinar that's pitching your product, you'll want to use a story about you or a client in *the Leap* stage to get them off the fence.

Conclusion

The Crossroads Formula is a perfect tool to beat writer's block because it gives you simple guidelines to follow to tell your own story. Not every story needs to cover every stage of the Crossroads Formula to be effective. But it's important to always keep your audience in mind when crafting stories and speak to the questions the members might be asking themselves as they're listening.

The Crossroads Formula is a useful template, and I invite you to refer back to it while reading the later chapters. Think about how you can use it to tell better stories inside your marketing and sales systems.

I've also developed a handy infographic that outlines all the stages of the Crossroads Formula in a charming and colorful layout. Many people like to print it out and place it on the wall near where they do their writing for quick and easy reference. You can download it and all the other resources in this book at resources.sellingwithstory.co.

Key Takeaways

- The Crossroads combines the best of the Hero's and the Buyer's Journey into a simplified framework.

- Your audience experiences your story as if they were living it, so tell a story that speaks to their mindset, desires, and fears.

- Use the Crossroads to tell a full story, or to tell just the right short story within your marketing, teaching, or sales.

CHAPTER 5

How to Use Visuals to 10x Your Storytelling

Visual storytelling is the art of creating a narrative through visuals that both engages and empowers your audience and also drives growth for your business. This tool is subtle and often overlooked in telling a story. Visual storytelling is an essential tool for anyone using writing, video, or speaking to enhance your story and communicate more information and emotion in less time.

In this chapter, we'll look at why visual storytelling is an essential tool for marketers to master and provide some down-to-earth strategies to help you get started telling better stories today.

Before we dive deeper into this chapter, it is important to note that the topic of visual storytelling is one that begs for lots of examples of video, high-resolution and color images, and animation. Obviously, books aren't the best medium to share examples like this. So bear with me as I do my best to describe and elaborate on the concepts here. If you would like a more comprehensive read, rich with examples and links, check out the reading list at resources.sellingwithstory.co.

Why Visual Storytelling?

As I've mentioned before, humans are not completely rational creatures. Strong emotions, not information, are what drive our decisions. When presented with "factual" information alone, only a small part of our brains respond. Wrapping information in a story can dramatically change how we process and interpret that same information.

In the movie *Inception*, Dom, played by Leonardo DiCaprio, is a kind of spy who can enter people's minds through their dreams and discover their secrets. In the movie, he's given an even bigger challenge: not discovering a secret, but planting an idea in their minds and making the individuals think they came up with the idea themselves.

That's every marketer's dream, but luckily for you, there's a way to do it in real life (and with a lot fewer car chases and gunfights).

Visual storytelling can make subtle cues in the minds of your audience members and inspire the right ideas, emotions, and desires to get them to take action.

How Our Minds Respond to Visuals

Visuals don't just impact our memories, they may actually influence our decision making. Jan Brascamp, assistant professor of psychology at Michigan State University, conducted a study to answer just this question. What he found was that the visual cortex (the part of the brain that processes sight) can impact our decisions and perceptions without any help from the more "rational" areas of our mind typically associated with decision-making.

"That is one sense in which our study is counterintuitive and surprising . . . The part of the brain that is responsible for seeing, for

the apparently 'simple' act of generating the picture in our mind's eye, turns out to have the ability to do something akin to choosing, as it actively switches between different interpretations of the visual input without any help from traditional 'higher level' areas of the brain."

Another study conducted by Laura Smarandescu at Iowa State University examined the habits of children at a summer camp for kids with diabetes. They found that showing images of a salad on their lunch menu dramatically increased how frequently salads would be ordered.

*"They found salad consumption among kids increased as much as **90%** when a digital display showed a rotating image of the salad."*

How to Determine the Right Visuals for Your Audience

Your visuals will only be as successful as their alignment with your audience's mindset.

A big-budget infographic conveying a sense of "luxury" may not perform as well as a minimal whiteboard video to a group of practical "bootstrappers" in the early stages of their businesses.

Know the Goal of Your Visuals

Your visuals should support a goal you want to achieve. Once you understand your goal, it's easier to determine what emotions and messages you want to convey to support the action you want your audience to take.

- **Tell your personal story** - Show your audience you're

relatable and human. Personal images and vulnerability are important here.

- **An inspirational manifesto** - Get people excited about your big vision for the world. Employ high-energy, bright colors and lots of movement.

- **A practical "how to" guide** - Teach someone something useful. Use minimal and practical visuals that help clarify and reinforce your points.

- **Product promotion** - Get people excited about your upcoming launch. Convey a mixture of pain related to their current problem and the opportunity for a better life once it's solved.

Where and How Will Your Visuals be Seen?

Understanding where and how your visuals will be seen can help determine what you want to create. This will help create boundaries that will inform your creativity and ensure your visuals serve the right purpose.

If you're doing an ad, a short 30-second video might be better than a drawn-out one. A visual to support your copywriting on a landing page could look very different from the image you use to promote that same page across social media.

The same visuals may have wildly different responses across the different social media platforms. Each of the major platforms (Facebook, Twitter, Instagram, LinkedIn, Pinterest) all serve different purposes to its users. You want your visuals to align with the platform they'll appear on.

What Are Your Strengths?

When creating visuals, you want to play to your natural strengths where possible. This will ensure you don't burn out creating stories you don't enjoy.

This goes beyond just your skills in the visual arts, however. Try to examine your other skills (data interpretation, a unique story, personality traits, your philosophy and beliefs) and consider the best mediums to let those qualities shine.

Set the Mood

Visual storytelling cuts right through our logic to the emotional centers in our brains. Because of this, you need to be deliberate in which emotions you want to stoke in your audience's heart.

Think carefully about what stage of the *Crossroads Formula* they are in, and which emotions they're feeling right now. What can you do to validate, empower, and inspire your audience?

What is Your Budget?

Be realistic about your budget and what is sustainable for your business to create.

High-quality video with lots of footage, music, graphics, and energy will be expensive, but it could be worth it if the video is for a big product launch or a high-ticket sales page. However, that same investment may not pay off for weekly blog content.

It's easy to get hung up on "the cost" of visuals and avoid it altogether until that "someday" when you "finally have enough" to invest.

Remember that with storytelling, budget and production is only a tiny factor in the bigger picture. What's more important is the alignment of the message. There are options for every kind of visual at every budget that you can take advantage of.

I'll share some tools at the end of this chapter to help you create effective visuals.

Choose Authenticity Over Perfection

This is an important point to follow up the budget. Visual storytelling does not need to be expensive and perfectly produced to be effective. Real stories that allow you to be vulnerable and authentic in front of your audience will always outperform big-budget projects.

A great example of very basic yet successful visuals is the Wait But Why? blog. This blog is one of the most popular online right now for its thoughtful and detailed articles about many of life's quirks and challenges. The author, far from DaVinci in his artwork, makes his own simple stick-figure cartoons and diagrams for every article. Though he won't be winning any art competitions with his work any time soon, his authentic visuals have been seen by millions. Though he could very well afford to hire a brilliant designer to help him, he continues with the simple drawings because of the endearing connection they make with his audience.

Be Consistent

We've already discussed how visual storytelling can help your message stick in the memory of your audience. But if you keep changing your story and your style, you'll end up working against yourself.

You want to be consistent so that the images, emotions, and ideas you share will become associated with *you*. Get clear on your tone of voice, the message, and the meaning behind your visuals through your marketing.

When to Use Visual Storytelling

Visual storytelling can be a useful tool whenever your audience needs to make a decision. This means there's a place for storytelling almost any time you come into contact with your audience. The trick is to decide early what decision you want to speak to in your story.

Though it's unlikely your audience will explicitly ask themselves these questions, it's something they're subconsciously doing all the time:

- Why should I keep reading/watching this?

- Should I download this resource?

- Should I sign up for this webinar?

- Do I trust this person?

- Should I buy this product?

- Should I click through this email?

Since we're almost always challenged by our audience with one of these questions, we can use visual storytelling techniques to help them find the answer on their own.

Where to Use Visual Storytelling

Supporting Graphics in Written and Video Content

The simplest and most obvious place to start practicing your visual storytelling is inside your content. It's never been easier to create interesting graphs and find powerful images that support the ideas and statements we make in our content. Adding images to your written copywriting can enhance your words and keep people engaged on your sales pages. Adding a few visuals to a video can add variety and intrigue to what you share on camera and avoid the "boring talking head" effect that happens.

Supporting Visuals for Your Talk

The best talks that get results for the speaker and win the hearts and minds of the audience only lightly leverage slides. This is especially true in the beginning and end stages of the talk where you're sharing a personal story and connecting with the audience, as opposed to sharing information. The speaker tells an engaging story that immerses the listener in an experience.

The slides are there to provide striking visuals which enhance the story. These usually have very little, or no, text, but they provide images of conflict, contrast, and emotion that follow the story.

Of course, during the section of your talk where you teach, you should use visuals as examples, testimonials, and charts and graphs to support your points. Avoid text-heavy slides when possible; instead, try to use visuals to eliminate the need for text.

Webinars

There are a few places where visual storytelling is more effective and needed than webinars. The same strategies to use for visuals for a talk will apply to webinars, but are even more essential, since people will mostly be looking at your slides.

Most webinars end in a call to action that requires a decision from your audience. Visual storytelling keeps your audience's attention through the webinar and helps them experience the key emotions along with the essential information they need to know to trust you.

Social Media

Creating strong visuals for our content, talks, and ads also translates into good bite-sized content, perfect for social media. By applying good visual storytelling principles to what you create, you'll be able to create a visual story with only one image or a short video.

The strongest platforms for visual storytelling on social media are currently Instagram, Facebook, and Pinterest.

Ads

Visual storytelling is essential in ads because you have a very limited number of words you can use. You need to rely on visuals to really make the emotional impact and get your audience's attention.

Email Series

It's 2018, yet we still, for the most part, use plain text emails as we did in 1998. If you're going to invest heavily in your visuals in your content, ads, and social media, why not use some of it in your email marketing as well?

All of the common email marketing tools allow for images to be embedded in your emails. There are a few specialized tools which allow you to embed videos in your email that can have some unique advantages.

Though it's certainly possible to add visuals to email, this is one I would recommend testing for its effectiveness before fully committing. Visuals can impact the deliverability of your emails, and plain text emails can often outperform emails with lots of visuals in certain cases. I recommend running a few marketing experiments to see how your audience (and the spam filters) responds to visuals in an email.

We'll explore some of these tools in a later chapter.

Landing Pages

Think of someone scrolling down your landing page like someone flipping through the pages of a book. Can you connect the visuals you use to create a story as someone progresses down your landing page? With visual storytelling, you can create a sense of progress that can inspire the right ideas and emotions to get your readers to take action.

Take a look at this example from Intercom:

This simple story shows how their product translates a complex problem into a simple and easy solution. These visuals drive the point home more than a block of text could, and the different characters and their expressions help create a sense of *before and after* that creates a story.

My Favorite Tools for Visual Storytelling

I'll give you a brief overview of a few of my favorite tools for visual storytelling here. For links and easy access to all of these, I've put together a tools list at resources.sellingwithstory.co.

Canva - This is the foundation for anything visual. This tool has everything you need, including free stock photos, nice fonts, templates, graphics, icons . . . and much more. This tool is a godsend for bootstrappers, and it's incredibly easy to use.

The only complaint I have is that it tends to create images with very big file sizes, so make sure you optimize your images for fast loading times.

I use Canva for almost all featured images that I create for my blog, podcast, and ads.

Over - This is a free (with paid features) mobile app that has some powerful layering tools to blend your text and images. This is an app you can pick up right away and start making some interesting visuals, but you can keep uncovering and learning to use new features and tools to create some impressive work.

Splice - This mobile app brings powerful video editing software to mobile devices. It makes it easy to string together videos, trim clips, and add sound effects and music. With this tool, all you need is a smartphone to start creating great video, so no more excuses!

Giphy Capture - This free app allows you to make your own animated GIFs quickly and easily. Animated gifs can be useful far beyond goofy memes (although those certainly have their uses). You can use them to demonstrate workflows and change.

Note that this tool is only available on Mac devices. If you're a Windows user, look for ScreenToGif.

Inkspace - For anyone who loves drawing, this tool will be a life-changer. This is free software that can turn your sketches into editable vector files on your computer. You will, however, need more robust software like Photoshop or Illustrator to work with the files after you have them on your computer.

Conclusion

As you undoubtedly know by now, visual storytelling is an incredibly powerful tool for big businesses and bootstrappers alike. Like many worthwhile skills in life and business, visual storytelling is something that is easy to pick up, but difficult to master.

Get started by focusing on a few key areas in your marketing where you could test out visual content. Don't try to apply all these ideas at the same time. Pick a specific concept, tool, or strategy to master first.

Over time, your visual storytelling will help you rise above the noise, connect with your audience, and get the full value out of your own unique story.

Key Takeaways

- People process visuals 10 times faster than text. Use visuals to enhance your stories and play on key emotions.

- You can use visuals in almost any marketing channel to create more engaging stories and content.

- Real stories and visuals that allow you to be vulnerable and authentic in front of your audience will always outperform big-budget projects.

CHAPTER 6

11 Storytelling Strategies for Better Sales

In the last chapter, we covered storytelling frameworks, which help you see the big picture in your storytelling. Before that, we covered some ways you can discover and uncover your own stories. We've covered a lot of ground, but you may still find it hard to take your stories and turn them into the powerful tools that drive sales.

In this chapter, I'm going to equip you with some storytelling strategies that should help close the gap. These are simple methods you can use to create compelling stories that keep your audience's attention, no matter if you're communicating through writing, video, podcasting, or speaking from the stage.

Tips for Opening Strong

In the first few moments (seconds in some cases) of your story, you must earn the attention of your listeners. They need to know why this story is important or interesting to them right away. Here are a few ways you can capture their attention immediately.

1 - Start Your Story in The Middle of a Conflict

A powerful way to open a story is to start in the middle of a conflict. The tension immediately grabs the attention and curiosity of your audience. The audience becomes invested in your story right away because of all the questions that pop up—how did they get into this situation? What happens next? It's tempting to try to lead into a story so you can explain the series of events that led to the conflict you're in, but you'll often lose them before you can really hook them.

See how you can open your stories on a cliffhanger, at the peak of an argument, at a rock-bottom point or putting out a fire (literally or figuratively). Give them just enough detail to know the stakes and then fill them in on the backstory as you go.

2 - Take Them Into the Room With You

When telling a story about yourself or one of your experiences, instead of describing it as something in the past, tell it in the present tense. Describe the sensations, thoughts, and ideas as if you were experiencing them for the first time in that moment. Instead of directly talking about how you felt or what happened, give little details that help us experience the story with you.

"The beeping of the machine in the hospital room . . . "

"I catch a trace of lilac perfume as she sits down."

"I feel the crunch of broken glass on the floor."

"I know I'm home just by the smell of Mother's fresh baked pie."

This transforms your story from a listing of facts to an immersive experience your audience shares with you as you tell it. This helps your audience relate to you more personally as they share the experience with you. Better yet, it will keep them from reaching for their phones because they're lost in the moment with you.

3 - Keep it Minimal

Every character, detail, conversation, or happening in the stories you tell should move the story forward in a consistent direction. Every unnecessary detail or point you make can distract from the purpose of the story, or leave your audience confused (meaning they'll check out). Cut out everything that does not reinforce your main point.

That may mean cutting details, which may feel like you're destroying your story, but it's setting you free to focus on what's truly valuable about the story you're telling.

A good exercise to get down to the bare bones of your story is to try to make it as small and simple as possible. Think about what idea you want your audience to come away with and then see how you can arrive at that idea in as few words as possible. Then do it again and cut your word count in half.

Tips for Creating an Authentic Connection With Your Story

Remember, the whole purpose of a story is to show your audience why you care about them and their problems. With a human connection comes more trust in your process and the ability to create results.

4 - Be Honest and Vulnerable

If you only talk about your successes, when you were right, or all your amazing victories, you'll come off as a hype marketer. This is poison for the long-term trust you want to build for your audience.

Being honest about your doubts, fears, feelings, and mistakes makes you human and relatable to your audience. They want to listen to someone they can relate to.

5 - Show Them What's at Stake

Everyone loves an underdog. It helps us see the human aspect of the characters in our story. It helps us relate to the adversity they face and understand what's on the line for them. The longer the odds, the more we care.

Tell us what's on the line in your story. We need a reason to root for the character. What happens if he fails? How are the odds stacked against her? For your audience members, this means what's at stake for them? They need to know what they can lose if they don't take action, not just what they gain if they move forward with you.

If you're a marketer, this could be revenue. If you dig a little deeper, this could be the difference between success and failure for the company. Or a new hire and a layoff.

If you're a doctor, this could be a life filled with pain, medication, and uncertainty, or a life of full potential, happiness, and presence.

As a financial advisor, this could be the difference between having money to pay for your kids' college or leaving them with only debt as an inheritance.

There is a careful balance to keep with this; you don't want to overdo the fear or potential loss too much. This can come off as salesly or inauthentic. But just a little pinch of this, like a little bit of cream in your coffee, can make your story more delicious and engaging.

6 - Validate Your Audience

The top reason people share content is that they want to communicate something about themselves to their friends. To get people sharing your story, you must speak to the qualities your audience wants or sees in themselves.

Your stories should help your audience make the statements they've always wanted to make but have never been able to find the words. Tell stories that allow your audience to better define themselves and grow relationships with other like-minded people.

Tips for Building Sales into Your Stories

We discussed building sales into your story in Chapter 2 - Grandma's Lasagna. We'll build on those concepts with a few more strategies to build desire so that, when you start talking directly about your products and services, your audience is already interested in moving forward with you.

7 - Tell Stories That Address Objections

The best stories directly address the common objections your audience will have. They provide a way for you to talk about the objections in a non-threatening and non-salesy way.

Take some time to write out all the objections you encounter when selling your products and services, or when teaching your process. Write direct objections to the product (It's too expensive; I don't want to learn a new tool.) and to your process (I don't have time to do this; I don't have a big email list; I don't have the "tech" background; I don't think I can change.). With these objections written out, start to brainstorm stories of clients (or from your own life) that show success in contrast to the objection.

Think about when these objections might come up in the minds of your audience when listening to you teach, or considering purchasing from you. With practice, you can time these stories so that you tell them right as they emerge in the minds of your audience.

8 - Focus on What's Interesting to the Audience

A common trap for stand-up comedians who hang out with a lot of other comedians is that they often start to pander to the other comedians in the back of the venue instead of focusing on the audience. They get laughs from the back, but the joke doesn't land with the majority of the room.

Many experts (especially marketers) get hung up in this same trap. Since we spend so much time in our fields of expertise and around other experts, it's easy to assume that everyone understands the jargon we use, and has the same level of interest in the details of our work. This is especially bad when we're at events and conferences and someone asks, "What do you do?" We vomit up a ton of useless information.

It's essential to have the pulse of the audience you truly want to reach and what they find interesting and engaging. Think about the results they want and put it in language they understand. You also don't need to cover every detail and aspect of what you do right away. Give them just enough information to understand and want to know more.

Consider these two things a health and wellness expert might say:

"Because of this genetic mutation, your methylation is off, so you can't process B vitamins efficiently."

Or . . .

"Because of this genetic mutation, if you eat certain kinds of food you're going to feel more fatigued and anxious than the average person."

One is entirely built around a practitioner's perspective, and the other focuses on the experience and desires of a patient/client.

9 - Leave Your Audience Wanting More

Though a resolution is something we ultimately seek in our stories, giving away too much in your story means you lose the audience's attention and imagination. This is a careful balance to keep; when telling a story, you want to give them enough information to get a "quick win" and feel empowered. If they feel like they've learned everything they can from you, they won't want to go deeper or buy from you.

Show the whole process, but go deep on just one aspect - When telling a story, give an overview of the big-picture problem and the road map to fix it. But instead of carrying them down the whole process, give them one or two steps to make some progress. Then after they feel like they've made some progress, remind them how much further they have to go, and how you can help them.

Give them a new step - Have you ever heard of "happily ever after" in real life? It doesn't happen. Every time a problem is solved in life, it makes room for at least one new problem to replace it. So instead of completely resolving your stories, give your audience an opportunity to take another step by hinting at what problems may come next.

You also want to make sure when you teach that your audience does not feel like they've learned everything they can from you. If that happens they won't see the value in moving deeper with you and purchasing your products or services.

10 - Create Big Goals for Your Business

A good tool for creating big goals that drive a story for your business is called a BHAG (Big Hairy Audacious Goal). This can serve as a focal point for all the work you do and creates something everyone (you, your team, and your customers) can get behind.

A BHAG is a goal that creates something bigger than yourself or the day-to-day business and allows you to discuss your passion, vision, and the reason "why" you're doing the work you do in the first place. Instead of just buying another tool or hiring another service, your BHAG can give your customers a sense of participating in your vision and making a positive impact on the world.

Connect your BHAG with your personal story and show why you care so dearly about this particular goal by sharing something from your past or present.

Make your goal something measurable and have a deadline, so you can track and report on your progress.

Here are a few examples:

- Help millions of people get the manager they deserve. - Jhana

- We choose to go to the moon in this decade and do the other things, not because they are easy, but because they are hard. - John F. Kennedy

- I want to help 100,000 entrepreneurs double their sales with integrity and love and zero ickiness! - Superhero Sales Academy

11 - Bake Social Proof Into Your Stories

If you just list off your highlight reel of clients you've worked with, results you've gotten, and achievements you've made, then you risk coming off as self-promotional.

You can avoid this trap by baking social proof into your stories. Use your social proof and case studies as teaching points. If your audience sees what you're talking about as educational instead of salesy, then they will lower their guards.

Instead of bluntly saying, "I helped a business grow to seven figures with content marketing," try building a story around it. "I learned a great deal working with WP Curve. But I think the thing that really helped us get to seven figures using just content marketing was focusing on our processes . . ."

Using social proof like this draws the attention of your audience and gets them interested in the result.

Conclusion

The strategies above should help you hone your personal stories into powerful and compelling narratives that move your audience closer to you. Some should be easy for you to understand and apply to your story; others may take practice, refinement, and possibly even coaching to become what you want them to be. Don't try to work with all of these strategies right away; pick the ones that make the most sense for your story, and you can slowly work your way through the others.

Be patient with yourself and diligent with the process; working with your own story can be emotionally and intellectually challenging. The best storytellers have spent many years honing and perfecting their stories. You can get there, too, but don't try to compare what you have to others at this point.

Key Takeaways

- You only have a few minutes to make a strong impression and convince your audience you're worth listening to. So open strong.

- Be authentic and vulnerable in your stories to create that human connection and build trust.

- You can embed social proof, mentions of your products, and share big goals for the impact you want to make on the world to build more sales into your storytelling.

PART II

One Clear Lesson

Well done!

If you've read through all of Part I, then you're on your way to creating your One Clear Message! This is the most challenging part of the process. The rest will fall into place easily. You may have to learn some new tools and technology in this section, but now you have a clear focus on where you are going and what your goals are.

Your message gets the attention of the people you want to serve. Your next step is to educate and empower them.

With the right lesson, you can change the beliefs, mindset, and lives of your audience. Shifting the foundational beliefs about what's possible for your audience can transform even the staunchest skeptics into raving fans.

One clear lesson can create superheroes.

Becoming Dr. Z

Before he was transformed into Dr. Z, Chris Zaino was a trainer and bodybuilder. He was great at what he did and had a Mr. Universe trophy to prove it. But he also had a secret he was trying to hide behind his strength and success.

He has ulcerative colitis. I'll spare you the details, but it's an autoimmune disease that can be terminal and is definitely no fun. The disease took him from 230 pounds to 160 in a matter of a few months, destroyed his energy, his self-image, and left him unable to have children.

He sank everything he had into finding help. But after over a year of seeing specialists, taking medications, and various procedures, he wasn't making any progress. The doctors he worked with told him his last option was to remove a large portion of his lower intestine. This plan did not have a very high success rate. With a huge risk for infection and cancer, he would need to spend a year in ICU, and his quality of life going forward would be significantly lower with medications and a colostomy bag.

This was not the vision this ultra-competitive bodybuilder had for his life. But what could he do? He did everything the doctors had told him to do, and it didn't work. His genetics had betrayed him, and medicine had failed him.

While Chris was pondering pulling the trigger on this last-ditch effort of surgery, an unexpected friend, an anatomy teacher from high school, approached him and told him he should go see a corrective care chiropractor he knew.

"A chiropractor? Please . . .," Chris thought, a bit insulted by the suggestion. It was common for all kinds of people to suggest all sorts of different treatments, but how was someone who works with aligning your knees and stretching your hamstrings going to make a difference here? He politely declined and let his friend know he had tried everything.

His friend responded with a lesson that would change his life. "Chris, if you tried everything then you'd have your health back."

This hit him like a lightning bolt. He realized he had lost hope and given his power away. He decided he had nothing to lose and went to see the chiropractor.

The chiropractor found Chris' spine was twisted like a gnarled root, blocking his nervous and immune system channels from his brain to his lower body. Finally, with a ray of hope, Chris asked the question he'd been asking over and over for years,

"So, when am I going to get better?"

The chiropractor responded with another powerful lesson that would change the course of Chris' life. "Well, as long as there's this blockage and damage, you're not going to be in the environment you need to heal . . .," but he then pointed at Chris and said, "But when you choose to correct the problem that you have and that's affecting your future, then your body will be in an environment to heal itself and you'll get better."

The way this doctor spoke to him not only started a fire in Chris to take responsibility for his problem and heal himself, but to go on to study chiropractic medicine.

In true superhero fashion, this lesson transformed Chris Zaino into Dr. Z, who not only healed himself and restored his strength but also built the most successful chiropractic agency in the US. People flocked from around the country to seek his healing after being inspired by his story. He is also the father of two children, something the doctors told him would be impossible only a few years earlier. Beyond that, Dr. Z speaks across the country and has a coaching program called, *I Am Hero,* which helps people live their own superhero stories.

They've Got 99 Problems, You Solve One

Like the story with Dr. Z above, one good lesson can be life-changing, or in his case life-saving. You can do the same for your audience.

Whether you're working with health, business, relationships, or finance, your audience and your customers are facing problems. Whether it's improving your sales or overcoming disease, often when someone faces a problem for long enough, they start to believe they're a victim and won't be able to find a solution.

We often expect our clients and customers to immediately understand our value, but we don't meet them where they are in their understanding. They may have tried dozens of other solutions and been burned by all of them. They may feel disempowered by their circumstances. They may be telling themselves a very different story than what's real.

As the authority on the problem you solve, it's your job to empower and inspire your audience that they can solve this problem. They probably won't just believe you at face value and dive right into working with you. You need to educate them, provide them with insight and emotions that will change their minds and shift their paradigms.

Think of it like this: Your audience has hundreds, if not thousands, of problems to contend with, but they can only really focus on one or two at any given time. They'll choose which problem to focus on in one of three ways:

- The most painful

- The most potential gain

- The one they feel most empowered to solve

This is why education is such a crucial part of marketing and sales. It's not just your job to solve their problems, but to make them feel empowered to solve the problem. If they don't believe the problem they have can be solved, then they won't resonate with your message or your offer. They'll move on to an offer or idea that feels achievable to them.

What to Expect in this Section

In Part II of this book, we'll show you how to create your *One Clear*

Lesson that inspires your audience and how to build a system around this lesson so that you can share it at scale. We'll cover some of the more technical elements of the *One Clear Path to Sales*, such as tools, design, and automation. I've set this section up in a way that whether you're just getting started with web-tech stuff, you've got the basics handled, or if you're a tech genius, you'll get some value and inspiration from this section.

We'll also work on building the foundations of a system to allow you to sell your products at scale. Through the stories we tell and the lessons we teach, we'll start to build the desire for your product or service.

CHAPTER 7

Building Your Clear Lesson

Knowledge is power.

You've probably heard that phrase before. I partially agree with this. It's powerful only when used appropriately.

All your knowledge won't do you any good if you can't connect with those who can benefit from it. It's like keeping a Picasso painting covered up in your attic.

Many entrepreneurs are hesitant to share their knowledge with their audiences before they become clients. They fear if they share their brilliance, nobody will want to work with them, because they already know everything you've got and can do it on their own. Others seem to open the floodgates at any opportunity, drowning their listeners in information.

But sharing your knowledge in a clear lesson can build trust and excitement with your audience. Through education, they can learn how you get results for your clients, what makes you different, and why you're the best person to help them solve their problems.

In this chapter, we'll discuss the essential framework and strategy for creating your one clear lesson and how to teach in a way that gets people excited to work with you.

Coming Up with the "Big Idea" for Your Lesson

It's time to put all the work we did in Part I researching our audiences, their mindsets, and the stories they're living and connect all this with a message that will capture and keep their attention long enough for us to teach them. The first step is to come up with a *big idea* to build that message and lesson around.

The father of advertising, David Ogilvy, once said:

"A big idea is an idea that is instantly comprehended as important, exciting, and beneficial. It also leads to an inevitable conclusion, a conclusion that makes it easy to sell your product.

"You will never win fame and fortune unless you invent big ideas. It takes a big idea to attract the attention of consumers and get them to buy your product. Unless your advertising contains a big idea, it will pass like a ship in the night."

The Three Key Ingredients to a Big Idea

So how do we create something so memorable, so compelling? It usually boils down to three ingredients:

- **Contrarian** - Does your big idea challenge commonly held beliefs and behaviors around the problem?

    o Example: The Ketogenic Diet - while decades of transitional diet wisdom encouraged low-fat diets to lose body fat, the Keto diet encouraged eating a lot of fats for better results. Which captured the hearts of bacon enthusiasts around the world.

- **Easy to understand** - The value of your big idea must be immediately recognizable and tangible to your audience.

  o Example: *The 4-Hour Workweek* - The bold title of Tim Ferriss' book instantly hits on a big desire and a clear promise.

- **Timeless** - Will your idea still be relevant in one, five, or 20 years from now?

Brainstorming Your Big Idea

It takes time, research, and experimentation to identify the "Big Idea" of your lesson. Often the most challenging part is distilling the idea down to just a few words.

Start by writing out a few compelling desired outcomes for your audience. Once you have a few listed, look at the common beliefs and behaviors people have to get that outcome. Can you challenge those? Do some freewriting around this and get the thoughts out of your head onto the paper.

After you've got some material to work with, try to rewrite the idea in as few words as possible, without taking the edge off the contrarian idea or the value.

Once you've got your big idea identified, you're ready to start building your lesson around it.

Five Keys to Successful Presentations

There's more to teaching than just sharing information. Successful teaching results in successful understanding and learning; otherwise, you are not teaching, just talking. You need to make the information relevant to everyone listening. More importantly, you need to balance teaching information with building desire to move deeper with your products beyond this lesson. Let's explore some of the key elements.

1 - Build Your Presentation Around Your Process

In Part I, we discussed creating a proprietary process for how you get results. A great process not only makes it clear how you do what you do, but also makes it easy for others to do the same. In your One Clear Lesson, you don't have to teach your whole process; you can share one step or a high-level picture of your process. You can show them your whole process and what the ultimate result is, but just teach them how to take the first step.

A good presentation usually has three to five teaching points that address specific beliefs or problems related to your process. You show them how the commonly held belief or solution is wrong, and what the new belief should be. Give a story, metaphor, or case study to illustrate your point.

Here's an example process a productivity coach may use to help entrepreneurs work less but earn more.

The 4-Day Weekend: How To Work Less But Earn More

1. Cut The Busyness - Cut out tedious, repetitive tasks.

2. Find Your Superpowers - Identify the activities that are driving the most revenue for your business and make more time.

3. Handoff - Delegate anything you do that's not a superpower.

Here's a quick example of what that productivity coach/consultant may say while teaching:

"A lot of people believe they need to work harder to make more, but I believe the opposite. I'm going to show you why working less may actually help boost your income. A client of mine, Deborah, actually doubled her income while cutting 10 hours from her workweek. Here's what she did... [teaching] ... Most of her progress came from one simple step. Here's how you can almost instantly cut two hours from your workweek...[teaching]."

By giving them a little bit of information to make progress within your process, they'll start to desire your help to implement the full picture.

2 - Teach to Sell

On a webinar, there's a careful balance of selling and teaching that you need to maintain to successfully convert your audience to customers. You can't oversell; nobody is going to stay tuned to a webinar full of product-pitching with no value. But most people tend to err on the other side of the spectrum.

If you teach too much, you may leave your audience overwhelmed, or with a feeling that they can now go do what you teach on their own. This is a disservice to them because they likely won't invest in you, and it won't be as effective as it would be to work with you.

The balance is teaching to sell. Instead of teaching people *how* to do something, you teach them *what* to do and *why* it's important. This seems like a subtle difference, but it could be thousands of dollars of difference. So instead of going into too much detail on how to do things, giving people step-by-step guides to solve their whole problem, show them *what* is important to do, give them enough information to get them a quick win as we've discussed before, and share *why* this is so important for their success.

Here are a couple good and bad examples:

Someone offering coaching, products, or services to busy mothers.

- **Bad -** Many moms don't feel like they have enough time in the day to take care of themselves; here's my system to build self-care into even the most hectic schedule.

- **Good -** Many moms feel guilty taking time for themselves when they have so much else depending on them. I believe that taking care of yourself is the best way to take care of your loved ones. I'm going to show you why that is and give you one simple step to build more me-time into the week.

A financial planner who works with small businesses.

- **Bad -** Today I'm going to show you how to capture more profit in your business and how to turn it into long-term wealth.

- **Good -** Most entrepreneurs think revenue is the main measure of success for your business. Today I'm going to show you what really matters when it comes to the success of your business—your profitability. Today I'll show you why you need to focus less on revenue and more on profit, and I'll give you some great ideas on what to do with that extra profit to build wealth.

In both cases, the first just gives information, but does not address the deeper beliefs that may be the source of the problem. The second shifts beliefs about the problem, then gives the information in context of the new belief. Though it gives helpful information, it focuses more on teaching to change a belief, not give information. This helps the teaching sink in, builds trust, and positions you as the guide to help them explore their new beliefs.

3 - Give Them a Quick Win

Your audience is much more likely to move forward with you if they feel empowered. A good quick win not only inspires trust in you and what you do, but inspires trust in themselves and their ability to get the results you promise. Remember that they're likely frustrated and feel like they've tried everything, so any kind of progress can really fire them up.

You need to be strategic in what you choose to teach when sharing your quick wins. They need to be useful and actionable so your audience can experience the win and momentum, but it can't leave them feeling like that's all you have to teach. In your lesson, you should show them a big-picture result; the quick win is just a few small steps to get to that result. When you teach your big win, show them how it fits in with the bigger picture to help them imagine how great it will be having your help through the whole process.

Here are a few examples of some quick wins to help you:

- If you're a fitness coach who works with back pain, give your audience a few easy stretches they can do every day. Then let them know this is only one component of your coaching program.

- If you're a marketer teaching about email marketing, give them a tip to write better subject lines. Then show how it fits in with a bigger process.

- If you're a dog trainer, show them one sign their dog is about to misbehave and an easy strategy to correct it before it happens. Then show how it fits in with your whole "Who's a good boy?" masterclass.

- If you sell health/beauty or nutrition products, talk about one ingredient you use, its benefits, and some ways to use the ingredient on its own. Then talk about how you have this ingredient in your product, and how your formula supercharges the benefits of the ingredient.

4 - Give Them Short-Term and Long-Term Ideas

Though quick wins are important, if you only share "quick win" information, your audience will walk away from your content feeling like they've got everything you have to teach and won't feel drawn to work with you.

By teaching a mix of ideas and strategies that provide both quick wins and long-term wins, this will encourage your audience to want you along for the journey.

5 - Address All Relevant Skill Levels

If you only teach to the beginners or the experts in your presentation, you'll alienate the others in your audience who are more experienced. You want as many people as possible to identify with your teaching and the offer you'll share at the end of the lesson, so make sure you have ideas for everyone.

You also want to directly address all of your audience in your teaching with a statement called a *linear path to learning*. It calls out all skill levels in the audience and helps them identify with your teaching. Here's an example:

"Whether you're totally new to Facebook Ads, you're running some

campaigns, or you've got an agency spending thousands on ads every day, this lesson is for you."

One quick caveat to this: You want to address all the skill levels appropriate for your offer; don't worry about teaching those who are not your ideal customers. So when creating a linear path to learning, focus on the spectrum of ideal customers. This can also help you keep away potentially bad clients who would not be a good fit for you.

Creating Your Presentation

There are a few forms of content that are well suited for storytelling, scalability, and teaching. Depending on your audience, some of them may be more effective than others. I recommend starting with one, testing and improving it, then repurposing it into different formats. (I'll talk more about repurposing a little later in this chapter.)

Webinars

Webinars are online presentations that typically last an hour. This is where I recommend most people start building One Clear Lesson because they are the most versatile, easiest to create, and easy to get feedback on.

A webinar is a classic way many marketers will pitch their products or services. Usually, the webinar is dedicated to high-value content that clearly relates to the problem you solve, then near the end of the presentation makes an offer. Usually, you put a link up to a sales page with your special offer. (We'll discuss more about sales pages later in the chapter.)

They are structured and function very similarly to delivering a talk from the stage, but they come with extra challenges. It's more difficult to hold someone's attention on a webinar and get them to show up.

There are a few ways to keep people engaged and ensure they show up:

- Make sure you have a good webinar anticipation series setup that reminds people about the event and keeps them excited. (We'll talk more about these in the email automation chapter later in the book.)

- Offer bonuses like extra content throughout and also at the end of the presentation. Tell them about the gifts you're sharing at the beginning, or even in your anticipation series, so they know what to stick around for.

There are also two different ways to do your webinars.

Live Webinars

This is a webinar where you are live with the audience. Live webinars are recommended for people who are new to webinars or have a new webinar presentation they're still testing out. The big benefit to being on the webinar live is your ability to directly interact with the audience and answer specific questions.

Automated Webinars

Automated webinars are a powerful way to scale up pitching your products. You can take a high-performing presentation and run it on an hourly basis, even up to every 15 minutes. The big advantage here is that there's almost no waiting. You can lose a lot of people if they register and need to wait a few days for the webinar.

Combine a good automation with a steady source of traffic and you've got a cash machine. Paid Facebook advertising works really well with automated webinars. With clarity on who you are serving and targeting with your ads (see Chapter 3 on customer avatars), you'll be able to have a steady stream of webinar attendees on demand. This system, when perfected, can be the primary growth engine for a business.

Automated webinars require more tech expertise to manage, and your presentation needs to be excellent to get conversions. If you're going to send paid traffic to an untested webinar, make sure you start small and make sure your ads, webinar registration page, and offer are all converting well. I recommend the automated webinar strategy for those with high-ticket offers and with some marketing experience (or good help on your team).

Micro Books

A short book built around your process can be a powerful way to connect with your audience and build credibility. There's a power to having a physical product to give to people, especially if you're a consultant or coach who is mostly working in the digital realm.

A good micro book is usually 15,000–20,000 words and can be read in less than two hours. This makes it easy to consume and will keep you focused on only delivering the most essential information.

I originally set out to make this book a micro book... I failed because I could not resist the temptation to add more. To succeed where I failed, build your book around a quick win, or one step in your proprietary process.

A common mistake people make with books is they see them as a product in themselves. You don't want to try to sell your books as a product themselves or try to get a lot of book royalties. Instead, you want your book to set up your readers to take the next step with you. That means mentioning your product or service at the end of the book and providing extra content they can download so you can get their email addresses. With this strategy, you can be generous with your book and the information within, knowing in the long run it will attract customers to you.

Challenges / Mini Courses

Challenges are a series of content (typically videos) that you release over a series of days which help people with a certain theme or problem.

Challenges are great because they allow you to get quick wins for your audience over a series of days. Which can really build up trust and momentum.

Each day you need a core lesson and some homework of sorts for the participants to implement. There's a careful balance you want to keep here. It should be something easy enough to implement or take action on in a day, but challenging enough that they feel like they've made some progress.

Live / Social Media Challenge

The live challenge and all running challenges on social media can have a viral effect.

Having challenges live on social media means you can get more engagement from your audience and have them share some of their wins and takeaways. Having people share not only rewards those who are listening to you and taking action by giving them praise, but it also encourages others who have been silent or have not yet started to engage with you. You get an opportunity to get really personal with people and see who your message and your lesson is really connecting with.

Live challenges can be run by hosting a live call on software such as Zoom.us or using social media livestream tools like Facebook Live or Instagram TV.

Evergreen Challenge

An evergreen challenge sacrifices some of the interactivity of the live challenge but has the advantage of being more scalable. It could be the same content as the live challenges described above, but it's set up to be automated so anyone can take it at any time.

It's often best to run a few live challenges, and once you have them working well and converting reliably, then turning it into an evergreen challenge.

An evergreen challenge can be created by putting your challenge videos on a series of landing pages and then creating an email automation. (We'll talk more about those in later chapters.)

Repurposing Presentation

When I mention books and publishing to the clients I coach and work with, they often check out or get nervous. A book seems like a daunting and intimidating thing to create. Any of the types of content listed above can be challenging to create and take a long time to develop. The good news is, creating another piece of content from the scaffolding you've already made is much easier and can still create a lot of value.

With one of my clients, Dr. Grace Liu, we created a seven-day challenge called *Seven Steps To Heal SIBO*. SIBO is a health condition that's poorly understood and often misdiagnosed. She created a 30-minute video each day for seven days, giving a quick win each day.

Thirty minutes of content every day is a lot of information. I was able to take transcriptions of the videos from each day and distill it into seven easy-to-read chapters for a book. I also closed each chapter mentioning a free seven-day video companion course for the book, which turned the book into a lead generation tool.

So when creating your presentation, see if there are ways you can repurpose what you've worked so hard to build into a different medium.

Conclusion - Keep it Simple

The most common mistake I've seen in my experience with creating One Clear Lesson is overdoing it. It's hard to keep things simple when you have a ton of brilliance to share.

In his book, *The 4-Hour Body*, Tim Ferriss describes something called a "Minimum Effective Dose" or the smallest amount of work that creates a result. For example, water boils at 212°F at standard air pressure. Water is not "more boiled" if you add more heat.

How can you create a Minimum Effective Dose with your teaching? What's the least amount of information you can teach while still providing value? This is actually more difficult than teaching a long lesson. But honing in on what the Minimum Effective Dose is when teaching will help you master storytelling and interacting with your audience.

Having great teaching points will serve you whether you're on a sales call, livestream, podcast, speaking on stage, or wherever else you find you have your audience's ear. To make building your lesson easier and faster, I've created a *Process Builder Template* to guide you through building a key lesson around your process. You can download that at resources.sellingwithstory.co.

Key Takeaways

- The best presentation is created around a big idea that's contrarian, unique, and desirable.

- Teach enough to build confidence and desire, but don't teach so much that they feel they've learned everything they can from you.

- Once you've created a great piece of presentation, it's easy to repurpose it into different formats.

CHAPTER 8

What is a Sales Funnel and Why Do You Need One?

Isn't it strange how in grocery stores you always seem to wander from one end to the other? The butter seems to be on the opposite corner from the bread. So you cross the store, listening to that easy pop music and seeing every end cap with random impulse-buy products. By the time you make it to the bread, you've got a few things in your cart you never set out to buy.

There's a very intentional design to grocery stores. They're like casinos, meant to keep you wandering around and spending more time and money in their store. They actually try to make it difficult to get what you want, because if it was easy, you'd be in and out.

Many businesses take a similar approach to their web design. Their homepages offer dozens of products, pieces of content, and calls to action. But unlike grocery stores where people will patiently wander until they find the butter, they will quickly leave your site if it's not immediately clear you have what they want and how to get it.

People don't have the attention spans to sift through information and make decisions when browsing your site. Attention is a limited and extremely valuable resource that too few people take into account when they design their sites. Most of us want to show a visitor everything we offer for fear that if they don't see it, they'll never buy.

What people really want is to be understood, educated, empowered.

How can we create these feelings with our audience in a way that's scalable? This is where the idea of a funnel comes in. The funnel is the perfect tool to communicate to your audience and create a personal experience that's consistent and reliable. It's a way to take your brilliant teaching and to share that message at-scale, on-demand, and automatically.

In essence, a funnel is just a website, but instead of designing your website like the grocery store mentioned above, we build it to be more targeted and anticipate what our visitor wants, building a more curated experience around that. Whether it's to buy your product, to sign up for your email list, or join your membership area, a funnel focuses on clear next steps for them as you guide them to your best offers.

The goal is to create a single path with clear yet small steps they can take. With every step comes a little more education and a deeper solution to the problem. You start small with something free and easy to consume and then progress through more and more valuable and comprehensive offers if they continue to engage. This ensures everyone gets what they want; if someone just wants a freebie, they get it and they don't need to move further, but those who are thrilled to invest heavily in what you're offering will always have an opportunity.

How to Build a Sales Funnel

Sales funnels are usually made up of a few components. Sales and automation components like landing pages, sales videos, automated email series (or sometimes messenger bots) and content components like lead magnets, educational video series, articles, and sometimes more involved content like webinars and strategy calls. If you're not yet familiar with some or all of the things mentioned above, don't worry, we're going to cover most of them in the following chapter.

Start with What You Already Have

Remember, our goal right now is to get your sales as quickly as possible. A common trap people can fall into is trying to create all these components at once and burn out before anything starts working. There's a nice quote by Jack Cornfield that says, "Tend to the part of the garden you can touch." It was said more in the context of how you can improve your life and make an impact on the world, but it fits nicely with building your funnel.

There are endless models for funnels with upsells, downsells, and cross-sells, but a simple and effective model to start with has three components:

1. **First Contact** - Here, you are introducing yourself to your visitor and offering some free content in exchange for an email. Getting them to share their email is what allows the rest of the automation to do its thing.

2. **A Small Offer** - The next big milestone of trust is to get your visitor to make a purchase. So it's usually a good move to start with a relatively small offer before presenting a bigger one.

3. **Your Main Offer** - Your core offer of your business.

What do we do to move them between these stages? This is where the Crossroads Formula comes into play. This system aligns nicely with the know, like, and trust components of the formula, providing a map to follow the buyer's questions we need to answer with our story in order to move them between each stage.

Here's a basic idea of how it could play out:

First Contact (Know) - A visitor lands on your homepage and gets a call to action to download a free (yet very valuable) piece of content (This is usually your One Clear Lesson.). This content is directly related to the bigger problem you solve. It outlines some of your "Grandma's Lasagna" process and may show them how to do one step of it themselves. They get a quick win from this contact and feel a new sense of confidence and empowerment to solve their problem.

A Small Offer (Like) - They feel empowered by their quick win, but they also realize how much more there is to be done. If they're serious about getting the results they want, they need to invest in themselves to make it happen. You offer a product that can take them one step closer without breaking their banks. One of the biggest steps of trust someone can make with you is to make a purchase; whether it's $1 or $1,000, there's a psychological barrier that needs to be crossed.

Your Main Offer (Trust) - They've made a small purchase, shown they really want their problem solved and they trust you to help them. Now is your chance to present your main offer.

Let's explore a few examples of this in different industries.

A Home-Brew Kombucha Supply eCommerce Store:

First Contact - Your visitor arrives with a curiosity about brewing their own kombucha at home. They have no idea where to start. You have an ebook that outlines the whole process and points out the common beginner's mistakes.

A Small Offer - They finish their ebook and are ready to start brewing, but also see how involved the process can be. You offer a starter kit of supplies they'll need to have to make a basic, small batch of kombucha.

Your Main Offer - After making their first few batches of kombucha, they're hooked. You now send them a coupon for a discount on a single item in your store. They now understand the process of brewing and the equipment needed to navigate the dozens of items in your store without feeling overwhelmed or confused.

See this live at Kombuchakamp.com.

Self-Publish a Book Information Product:

First Contact - A compelling webinar that shows you how to write a bestseller in as little as 90 days.

A Small Offer - A self-publishing starter kit that helps you mind-map and outline your book idea. This small investment will get you started on the road to getting published with just a few select lessons pulled from the main course.

Your Main Offer - For those fully committed to getting their book published. A course that walks you through the full process of writing and publishing and becoming a bestseller on Amazon.

See this live at self-publishingschool.com.

A Podcast Production Service Business:

First Contact - You have a comprehensive guide for launching your podcast. You demonstrate everything necessary to have a successful podcast launch. It comes in the form of a simple checklist that's easy to follow and understand, but does not go too deep into the individual elements of it.

A Small Offer - They're hooked on podcasting. Maybe they've launched, maybe they're just starting their interviews, but they're committed. Your guide was helpful to show them the path, but they need more detailed guides to make sure they take every step properly. You offer a more comprehensive course that outlines podcast launches, management, and monetization.

Your Main Offer - They now know everything that goes into making and maintaining a great podcast, but it's a lot of work to handle it all. They now understand how valuable it can be for their business, though, and they're willing to invest to make it great. You've got a full done-for-you podcast production service that will take all the headaches out of the "behind the scenes" work of podcasting so they can just focus on interviewing great guests and creating amazing content.

See this live at fullcast.co.

A Health Coach / Remote Doctor:

First Contact - You specialize in helping people overcome a specific gut-health problem. It's poorly understood and often misdiagnosed. You have a short book and a seven-day challenge that gives a small step to overcome and manage this condition each day.

Small Offer - On the seventh day of your challenge, you mention you have a comprehensive course to help them understand and navigate the complexities of gut health. You offer extra value by including a bundle of blood tests and supplements personalized to them, so they get more than just static education.

Main Offer - You have a VIP one-on-one coaching service where you send supplements and run tests regularly to guide your patients back to health. The offer is expensive because your time is very limited and is not covered under traditional insurance, but by now your customers have gotten a taste of your expertise and finally see a light at the end of the tunnel for their health problems. Which makes it an easy investment for them.

See this live at healsibo.com.

Conclusion

The sales funnel removes the confusion that kills the sales of many brands online. It helps you build up the value of what you offer in the eyes of your potential customers before they ever see a price tag. Which transforms your main offer from sticker shock to a no-brainer.

This powerful process also simplifies things for you. Instead of trying to promote dozens of products, or discounting your services to get people to finally commit to you, you've got a single, reliable system that you direct people to that does the heavy lifting of sales for you.

Key Takeaways:

- Sales funnels can automate and simplify your sales process.

Once created and working well, your job becomes simple: get more traffic to it.

- Start with a smaller offer to open people up to the idea of being a customer. They'll often be more receptive to your high-ticket offers once they have made a purchase and feel good.

- Refer back to Chapters 1 and 3 on the Buyer's Journey to review the mindset of your audience as they progress through your sales funnel.

CHAPTER 9

Choosing Your Funnel System

In the last chapter, we explored what a funnel is and how it fits in with your business. In this chapter, we're going to explore some tools you need to create a sales funnel.

Before we go in and start to analyze the different tools, I want to empower you to make the best decision possible. You should do your own research beyond this chapter to figure out what will really work best for you, but here are the basic features you want covered:

- **Email Automation -** Emails that are sent out automatically based on how someone behaves (opt-ins, sales, clicks a link, submits a form).

- **Email Campaigns -** One-off emails that are broadcast to your whole list.

- **Integration -** Many businesses use dozens of different software tools; they should all be able to integrate and work together for the best results for you.

- **Landing Pages -** Web pages designed to serve a single

purpose (usually persuading someone to opt in or make a purchase) and combines text, images, and video to help persuade.

Before You Buy, Keep in Mind...

Switching costs: These tools can hook you stronger than sugar or cigarettes. Once you choose one and get set up, it's very difficult to switch to another provider. The longer you use one, the more costly it is to switch. This is a process that can take weeks or months and usually involves many headaches along the way. This is especially the case with landing pages, which you'll need to build from scratch all over again when switching tools.

So when you're choosing one, try to anticipate what your needs will be in a year or two, and choose a system you can grow into.

Scaling pricing: Most of these platforms start with a relatively low cost, but scale up as your email list grows. So try to imagine where you'll be in a year or two down the road and consider the pricing and features you'll want then. Once your list grows to 3k, 5k, or 10k and up, the price differences may seem insignificant compared to how much you're making from your audience, so try not to over-focus on price, even if you're a bootstrapper.

Integration: To get the most value out of these tools, they need to play nice with many other tools you and your team will use. Be sure to check if these systems integrate with other tools in your toolkit you're currently using.

Email Automation

The heart of a successful small business these days is a strong email automation system. These systems can do what 10 to 20 years back would have required a team of salespeople.

These systems serve up emails automatically to your subscribers based on how they behave on your site. We'll discuss more about email sequences in later chapters, but here's a few examples of what automation can do:

- If someone downloads a lead magnet, your automator has a series of emails to send them recommending your amazing product as the perfect next step.

- If someone is really engaged in your emails, your system can tag them and send them a coupon code for being such an awesome audience member.

- If someone has not opened messages or visited your site in a while, you can send an email with a more personal touch inviting them back.

There's a slew of email automation providers out there, and for the most part, they all do the same job quite well. I've listed three of my favorites below that I think will meet the needs of most of the amazing people currently reading this book. I have personally worked with each of these either on my own sites or on my clients' sites.

Each offer 14-day free trials (at least at the time of writing this book, but this changes often), which is enough time to get started on a few systems and get a feel.

ConvertKit

Pros: This tool is built specifically for bloggers and marketers. It's super simple to use, and it is easy to understand the analytics and metrics so you know when you're succeeding. They also claim they have the best deliverability in the business, meaning your emails don't get filtered as spam as much. It does have a landing page tool as well, meaning you may not need any other software for your funnel.

Cons: Can feel somewhat limited for more experienced marketers, especially if you want to use paid traffic. It also lacks some of the more robust integrations that other platforms on this list offer. Though there is a landing page builder included, it does not have many options and is limited compared to the landing page builders listed later in this chapter.

Active Campaign

Pros: The drag and drop. A really great, yet more sophisticated feature of Active Campaign is the conditional content. Meaning you can deliver a customized message based on a contact's gender, location, or pages they've visited on your site. It also has text message follow-up, which some may find handy.

Cons: Many of the features that set Active Campaign apart from the other providers are only available in the more expensive plans and may not be useful to most marketers.

Drip

Pros: This system is free for the first 100 subscribers. This is excellent for absolute beginners who are new to automation. If this is you, I recommend starting here, trying it out, and getting a feel for how these systems work. Once you hit your 100 subscriber limit, then do some research to choose the best tool for you while you've still got some switching ability.

Cons: Though it has the free plan, the lowest level plan comes in more expensive than ConvertKit and remains more expensive as you scale your list up.

A Quick Warning on Email Automation

Email automation is a very attractive and powerful tool, but like every powerful tool, it needs to be used wisely.

You will not be able to completely remove yourself from email automation without some drawbacks. Overusing automation can frustrate and push away your audience. Getting reported as someone who abuses email automation can impact the "deliverability" of your emails in the long run. Too many abuse complaints will mean your messages get caught in spam filters.

You should be making an effort to personally connect with customers or your automation will come across as stale, and you will lose touch with your audience.

There are also new laws being created (such as GDPR in the European Union) to regulate email automation and punish companies that abuse these systems.

Landing Page Builders

Landing pages are essential for creating funnels and sales on your site. Landing pages should serve a single purpose. Whether it's getting people to register for your webinar or purchase your coaching, a good-looking and compelling landing page is essential to successfully automate sales. (We'll talk more about how to make amazing-looking landing pages in the next chapter.)

ClickFunnels

This tool, though it includes email automation, is at its heart a landing page building tool. It's also worth noting that there are many in-house tools that you can upgrade to in your plan that integrate super smoothly.

Pros: This is a great all-in-one option for building funnels. It includes many templates not just for landing pages, but full funnels. Another fantastic feature is how easy it is to share funnels between users; if a friend or colleague has a well-functioning funnel you like, you can import the whole thing over to your account with a few clicks. This really is one of the most comprehensive and powerful tools on the market for funnels. It also has a really attractive affiliate program built in, which is pretty cool. Plus they have super good customer support!

Cons: It's the most expensive option on this list, you get what you pay for, but it can be a bit of a suffocating price point for early-stage bootstrappers. They push hard to upsell their tools. The affiliate program I mentioned above is awesome, but keep in mind anyone who is saying anything about ClickFunnels is probably an affiliate (even me); there's nothing wrong with that, but you should be aware. It's a tool designed for people and by people who are always selling.

Leadpages

This is simple, easy to use, and exclusively a landing page builder. Though it lacks the extra features of ClickFunnels, it does its core job (building great, high-converting landing pages) really well.

Pros: The drag-and-drop builder is very nice and easy to use. They've got a lot of nice-looking templates and are easy to start with and build on quickly. The templates are all mobile friendly, which is essential in this day and age. Their built-in leadbox system means all your opt-ins are two-step opt-ins, which help with conversions and keep your pages looking nice. You can also collect email subscribers via text message. It's much less expensive than ClickFunnels.

Cons: It is less expensive for a reason. While it does its job of building landing pages very well, it will require some integration and piecing together different tools to create a funnel. Their customer support is not as strong or responsive as ClickFunnels.

Optimize Press

This is a WordPress plugin and theme as opposed to an external tool.

Pros: This is the only pay-once tool in this list. The rest are monthly recurring fees. You keep everything in WordPress, and you keep ownership of your pages even if you stop using them (As soon as you cancel a subscription for the other tools, you lose access to the pages.). The tool is particularly well suited for membership sites.

Cons: This tool is only for WordPress. It's not as easy to use as ClickFunnels or Leadpages.

Conclusion

Choosing the right tools for you and your funnel system is not something to be taken lightly. It's entering a long-term relationship, so make sure you're partnering with tools that are a good fit for you. That being said, when you use these tools well it will be an extremely profitable relationship for your business. With the right story and the right system, you can dramatically simplify your marketing and sales work. You'll know where your leads are coming from each day and what to do to get more.

I've put together a short quiz that will recommend a system based on your needs and goals for your story funnel. This should help give you a little more guidance and insight into the decision. You can check out this tool at resources.sellingwithstory.co.

Key Takeaways

- It's very difficult to switch landing page and email automation software after you have been using it for a while. So make sure to choose a platform you can grow into. If you're just getting started with these tools, feel free to try a few.

- Remember, even with great automation, you should make an effort to personally connect with your audience.

- Be sure to check out the Funnel Chooser Quiz to help determine which funnel software is best for you.

CHAPTER 10

The Science of Design Hacking

As we learned in the earlier chapter about visual storytelling, stories go far beyond just words. Design is a crucial element of success when it comes to creating good landing pages, lead magnets, webinars, and all the other content you'll create in your One Clear Path to Sales.

Unfortunately, design is a difficult thing to do well. It can take years of study and practice to develop a good taste for design. Plus, just because it looks good to us does not mean it's going to convert. The goal of this book is to get you results fast, not send you back to school to get another degree.

Fortunately, there's a shortcut that can save you a few years and a few hundred headaches. It's called Design Hacking. There are many people out there who have invested thousands and thousands into good design. So instead of trying to reinvent the wheel, why not just see what they're doing well and adopt it on your own design?

I learned about Design Hacking from a close friend of mine, Kathryn Jones, who's a master at this process. Since I learned everything about this process from her, I thought it would be best to let her teach you in this chapter. The rest of this chapter is written by her, and though I'm sure you'll notice a slight change in her voice and writing style, I hope you'll find the pearls of wisdom she shares helpful. Over to Kathryn:

Looking Good is Being Good

"But, ugly websites sell more, right?"

I've gotten this question over and over again. To be frank, the answer is: no. Ugly does not convert. Ugly does not sell more. And, more often than not, ugly does not sell at all.

Now, rather than go into the details of how this myth started, I'm instead going to help you realize how this fact—being that ugly web pages sell more—is simply not true.

So, what is the truth?

The truth is that great design increases both your sales and your credibility.

Here's how:

- **Fact #1:** A Stanford University study states that people determine the credibility of your website in less than 0.5 seconds.

- **Fact #2:** This same study states that over 90% of what they're judging is your website's design.

The person leading this study was a professor named B.J. Fogg. He said, "Looking good is often interpreted as being good—and being credible."

Since the 1940s, social psychology research has shown that physically attractive sources (usually people) have been perceived to be credible sources.

"This is basic human processing bias—looking good is being good—also seems to hold true for evaluating the credibility of websites, especially since design look is highly noticeable."

- **Fact #3:** Humans have been communicating for nearly 30,000 years.

- **Fact #4:** But, written language has only been around for 3,700 years.

So, our brains are naturally hard-wired to process visual information better and faster than text.

In fact, our brains actually process visual information 60,000x faster than text, which checks out when you realize that people only read about 28% of copy on web pages.

There's a man named Dr. Brent Coker who studied the impact of attractive websites on human behavior. This guy is brilliant.

He says, "As aesthetically oriented humans, we're psychologically hard-wired to trust beautiful people. The same goes for websites.

"Our offline behavior and inclinations translate to our online existence. Websites that are more attractive . . . create a greater feeling of trustworthiness and professionalism in consumers."

- **Fact #5:** Salesmen are 43% more successful in getting people to buy when they use visual aids.

- **Fact #6:** The positive effect that great design has on consumers' buying habits is international.

For example, there was a study done in Singapore. In this study they found that participants were drawn to cleaning companies with green and a lot of white space (Usually, white space means empty space on the page, but in this case it's literally referring to the color white.) because that matched their idea of what is natural, fresh, and clean.

In contrast, these participants rejected cleaning companies that branded with dark colors because it appeared cluttered. Which is just honestly not what you want from a cleaning company.

You see, it's hard to sell online if you can't even get someone to stay on your site long enough to see what you're selling.

And, if they think your site is ugly, just imagine what they think about the quality of the products you're selling! If your site is ugly, people bounce. They're out of there.

A design facelift can help you not only increase your credibility (which increases your sales), but it also allows you to compete with the big companies.

If you look the part, you can play the part.

So, long story short?

If your funnel is ugly, you've already lost the sales game.

The Science of Design

Now, maybe you believe me. But, at this point, most people think, "Well, I'm not a designer. And, I certainly don't have $10k to $20k to fork over to a web designer. So, this will never work for me."

So, they compromise for an ugly webpage, an ugly funnel, lower conversions, and outdated templates. But, they sell themselves short. Because to have a high-converting design, you don't need to know how to code. You don't need Photoshop. And, you don't need any graphic design training.

Instead, you simply need to understand the science of design.

You see, I used to be one of these people—thinking that excellent, high-converting design was out of my reach. And, after $25k in internet marketing training and certifications, I still had no idea what to do.

That was, until I thought, "Hmmm, what would happen if I stopped approaching design as an art, and instead, as a science?"

Well, do you want to know what happened? Design hacking was born.

What is Design Hacking?

Design hacking is the process of strategically investigating the design and marketing processes of your competitors, which you then use to model and test within your own business.

In simpler terms, design hacking is swiping the design ideas of smarter, richer, and more successful businesses, and then using them for your own.

Now, why would you go to the trouble of doing all of this?

Because modeling success yields success.

Therefore, when you model your webpage or funnel to look similar to those of highly successful companies, you strip the sales secrets embedded within their design to use for your own business.

Now, is this legal?

Yes.

Isn't this stealing?

No.

Aren't there copyright issues at play?

Absolutely not.

Here's why: because we're not copying other people entirely. We're simply modeling them. It's the same reason why there can be two songs with the same chord progressions. They're not direct copies of each other, but the design model, structure, and design of the other.

Make sense?

So, what do you look for when you're looking to want to strip the design secrets of another site?

I'd like to introduce you to the SWIPES Method.

How to Use the SWIPES Method

The SWIPES Method is going to tell you what to actually look for when you find a design that you would like to hack. This is a simple way of examining the many different elements of design.

Let's break it down:

The first "S" stands for "STRUCTURE."

You're going to want to look at how this site is structured.

- **What do the sections look like?** - Look for how the big chunks of a page are structured. A section is usually big enough to fit the screen of a laptop and usually communicates a single idea.

- **How many rows and columns are there?** - Each section may have a series of rows and columns to organize the content on their page. Look for how many rows and columns there are, what information is contained in each, and what seems to catch your eye first.

- **How many sections are on the page?** - Is the page short and concise with just one section and a button? Or are there many different sections? What's the big idea in each section and what purpose do they serve?

Structuring your page similarly will yield similar results to their page.

Next, the "W." This stands for "WORDS."

What copy are they using? What fonts are they using? What is the style of the font? The size of the font?

The "I" stands for "IMAGES."

What types of images are they using? What is their placement? Are there background images? Foreground images?

"P" stands for "PAINT."

This is where you pay attention to the colors. What are the colors of the font? What are the colors of the background? What colors are they using to complement each other?

Next comes "E," which stands for "ENERGY."

Energy denotes anything on the page that *does* something. So, a button, a hyperlink, maybe a video that plays.

Pay attention to what—and where—they're using these Energy elements. Consider using the same for your own design.

Finally, the last "S" which stands for "SPACING."

How do all of these elements work together? How close are they? How far? Is there a lot of blank space or none at all?

When you go through this six-step process (S-W-I-P-E-S) to analyze any funnel or webpage, you're able to dissect what is happening within their design.

Following a similar pattern for your own will help you have similar success.

Three Steps for Finding Pages for Design Hacking

How do you know what pages to hack in the first place?

I invite you to consider these three questions:

1. What niche of business are you in?

If you are selling a product in the women's weight loss industry, hack pages of companies that are also selling in this niche. You can do a simple search for companies and businesses like this, or you can look in a few of these places that also serve your audience:

- **Podcasts** - Look for guests on the show and find links to their sites in the show notes.

- **Online Summits** - Look for speakers and their sites in their bios.

- **Conferences** - Look for speakers here, too.

- **Social Media Influencers** - Look for popular hashtags, topics, and communities.

2. Who are you selling to?

Find companies that are selling to your same type of customer. If your ideal customer buys from them, they will buy from you. Don't just try to hack people who sell the exact same thing as you; try to think a little broader about your audience and the many different problems they have.

For Example:

- If you sell ski boots, someone who sells jackets might also be good to hack.

- If you sell weight loss coaching, someone who sells cold-pressed juice may be a good model.

3. What do you want your customer to do?

If you want your customer to opt in for a free PDF, find web pages that are yielding that same result. If you want your customer to buy a $997 product, find web pages that are getting their customer to do the same thing.

Sometimes, the best pages you'll hack won't be listed on the home page. But you understand how funnels work and you can use this knowledge to uncover their offers.

Here's What I Mean:

- You can opt in to their email lists to see if they mention any offers.

- Download a lead magnet to see if they have an upsell on their thank you page.

- You may have to make a small purchase with them to see what they're offering beyond that. Buying a small $7 or $15 product for great design information is a great deal compared to a $10k web designer.

Conclusion

If you want to improve your sales, improve your design. If you want to improve your sales immediately, design hack.

By leveraging the work and money and research of other companies, and then applying those same principles to your own business, you can save yourself tens of thousands of dollars and months of time.

The guesswork is taken away because you're modeling design that has already been proven within your competitors' businesses.

So, use the SWIPES Method to start design hacking your competitors' businesses. The second you drive traffic to your site, you'll start seeing results right away.

Have fun designing. And, even more exciting—have fun with all the money you make from your improved design.

There's a deeper dive training in design hacking available at resources.sellingwithstory.co.

Key Takeaways

- A good-looking funnel is crucial for building trust and to position yourself as an authority.

- It's much easier to model your design after pages that are already successful than to figure out design by yourself.

- Modeling your sales funnel after those that are already working is 100% okay! Copying writing directly, using the exact same images, or stealing IP-protected content is not. As long as you're just modeling and adding your own essence to what you create, you'll be fine!

CHAPTER 11

How to Build Your List and Fuel Your Funnel with Lead Magnets

If you see a funnel as the engine that runs your business, then emails are the fuel to keep that engine running. All the messaging and communication you'll use in your funnel relies on getting an email address that people actually check. The best way to collect email addresses is with a lead magnet.

What is a lead magnet? It's a premium piece of content you offer in exchange for contact information from your audience. In many ways, a lead magnet is your first sale. Even though no money is being exchanged, you are asking visitors to trust you with their information and attention. These days people are careful where they share their contact information, which means your lead magnet really needs to shine to earn their trust.

In this chapter, we'll explore different types of lead magnets, how to make a winning lead magnet, and what you need to position and promote your lead magnets successfully. Equipped with this knowledge, you'll have an asset you can consistently use to drive traffic and attention to your story funnel.

What Makes a Winning Lead Magnet?

The importance of a good lead magnet for the success of your story funnel cannot be understated. If you can't get people into your funnel and in front of your offer, then there's no point in having an offer.

You want to make sure your lead magnet is attracting the right people to your offer. Attracting a bunch of cat lovers to your funnel that ends in an offer for dog training is a waste of time. It also serves the key role of warming your audience up to the offer you're going to make. By the time you make your offer, your audience should be clear on the huge value you provide and how this offer will get them what they want. Alignment with your story and the desires of your ideal customer is essential.

Here are a few key design principles to guide your lead magnet creation:

Make a Clear Promise

You should see your lead magnet as a product, which means you need to make a clear promise and address a desire your audience is feeling.

Your lead magnet design and messaging should be able to deliver a clear promise to solve a specific problem in the lives of your audience members.

The clear promise also removes a lot of the critical thought your audience members need to decide if they want to download it. If it's immediately obvious how they can use your lead magnet to get the result they want, they don't need to figure that out themselves. Many lead magnets never convert because they're simply too broad or vague.

Remember that the key promise you make in your lead magnet should fit in nicely with your proprietary process and clearly relate to your offer.

Give Your Audience a Quick Win

At any given time, a person (especially a business owner) has dozens, if not hundreds, of fires she needs to put out in her life. She'll choose one or two to focus on and then ignore the rest to conserve mental energy. She'll likely choose one of the following problems to work on:

- **The Most Painful -** If your hair is literally on fire, you won't be worried about "living with purpose" or contemplating your legacy. There's a painful problem that needs solving now.

- **The Best Opportunity -** People will focus on where they perceive the most opportunity for growth, profit, or impact would be.

- **The Problem They Feel Best Prepared to Solve -** People usually procrastinate on tasks they don't fully understand or know how they will handle. If they have a clear path to how they can solve the problem and feel empowered to do so, they'll take action.

A good lead magnet will address all three of these. It addresses a problem that's painful, potentially profitable, and transforms the steps they take from opaque and confusing to simple and straightforward.

Giving your audience a quick win with a good lead magnet will create the satisfaction of easing that pain and convince your visitor that the problem is both solvable and worth solving.

Best of all, a quick win sets your audience up to take more action with you. Someone who has just upgraded the problem you solve from "I'll get to it someday" to "Let's get this done" is much more likely to become a paying customer.

Keep it Short

We've already established that people have hundreds of problems gnawing at their minds every day, which means their time and focus is as valuable as their money.

Remember that money is not the only currency you're working with. Time, attention, and trust are also scarce. This means that the more time your lead magnet requires to be consumed, the more costly it is to your audience. Which means it's less likely they'll finish the lead magnet or even start it. Which ultimately weakens your funnel.

Embed Social Proof and Next Steps

A good lead magnet will use social proof to help encourage people to download it. But you can also bake social proof for your business into your lead magnet by adding case studies, testimonials, and facts about your business that will entice the audience to become customers.

Use stories about how you helped previous customers to support your key points and subtly demonstrate to your audience that you're a master at solving this problem and have helped many people solve it in the past.

Don't try to point at yourself with your social proof. Frame the customers you talk about in your stories as the heroes, keeping the focus on them and their results. The audience will make the connection on their own through your stories.

If you've followed the other advice in this section and built a lead magnet with quick wins, you're going to have people ready to go deeper with you. Though your lead magnet should provide a small quick win, it probably won't completely solve their problem.

This is why you should share some next steps near the end of your lead magnet. You've shown them what's possible and what it's like to work with you, so show them what the next level would be if they want to get serious.

This is often best paired with your social proof. Mention stories of customers who used your other programs and got great results. This allows you to talk about your services without being too salesy or pushy.

Types of Lead Magnets

There are many different types of lead magnets people use to capture emails. Each has strengths and weaknesses and some will be a better fit for your audience.

Though there are thousands of ways to make a lead magnet, we're going to focus on just four types that are easy to create and generally drive great results.

1 - Checklists and Cheat Sheets

A checklist can make for a great lead magnet because it guides people through a process (maybe your proprietary process). A checklist breaks down a complicated task into easy steps. Checklists are most useful when outlining a process that always follows a sequential set of steps. They can be used for something done once (setting up a profile on social media) or something that is done repeatedly (promoting a post on social media, or preparing for tax season).

A cheat sheet also helps your audience through a process, but the main difference is that a cheat sheet does not always have to be used in a sequence. Cheat sheets distill complex ideas into a simple and actionable format.

These kind of lead magnets are probably the easiest to create and don't require much of a budget to be successful. Many high-converting checklists can be as simple as a Google Doc or a black-and-white single-page paper.

If you're just starting to validate a business idea or a new product for your story funnel, consider making a checklist or cheat sheet to test your offer and funnel before you invest heavily in video or design for a lead magnet.

2 - Templates

Templates provide structure and frameworks that people can easily adapt to their own work. They're designed to save your readers time and to remove a lot of the critical thinking required to solve a certain problem. Templates save your visitor from having to "reinvent the wheel."

- Pre-written email templates and video scripts to make writing/filming easy.

- SOP (standard operating procedures) templates to delegate a task.

- Design templates to make building landing pages or other

content easy.

- Spreadsheets with functions set up to make it easy to manage data.

If you've read The Story Engine, you'll know this is a strategy I used inside the book itself. In many of the chapters in the book, I created a template to make it easy to take action on the concepts I outlined in the book. This makes it easier for people to take action and get a win with my content, and it has transformed Amazon into a source of traffic and lead generation for my business.

By far, the most successful lead magnet from that book has been the Content Strategy Template. This template alone has been responsible for thousands of new leads and still creates a steady stream each day. You can check it out at thestoryengine.co/resources.

3 - Interactive Quizzes

Quizzes are a powerhouse when it comes to lead magnets. To your audience, they're entertaining and insightful—they get to learn something about themselves and get personalized results.

This is also an ideal tool for those who have some sort of assessment as the first step of their proprietary process. You can use it to introduce people to the process and give them a few personalized steps to take on your process.

To you, they're not just a great lead-collecting tool, but an opportunity to learn more about your audience. Along with providing value, the questions that you ask in your quiz should set you up to get some insights into your audience. Use what you learn to create better content, come up with new products, and get a clearer picture of your audience.

Some quiz-building tools also offer "branching logic," meaning it adapts to how people respond to questions. For example, in one question on a quiz I created, I ask about the reader's skill level in SEO; if they respond, "I'm not so good at that," then an *Easter egg* question pops up offering to send them an article on SEO. This is a great personalized experience and boosts conversions.

If you'd like to take a look at this quiz, head to thestoryengine.co/quiz.

When to Use Lead Magnets Vs. Your One Clear Lesson

At this point, you might be asking, "Wait... I already have my One Clear Lesson figured out, and that's free, why can't I use that as my lead magnet, too?"

Well... Good question! Thanks for taking the initiative.

Lead Magnets are useful to offer as a gift when speaking on stages or podcasts (In these cases, your talk is your One Clear Lesson.). Often, trying to share a webinar or other teaching content where you make an offer at the end is forbidden from most speaking situations. In this case, give away your lead magnet to collect emails and create an email automation to follow up with them and encourage them to check out your One Clear Lesson as the ideal next step.

So when would we offer our One Clear Lesson first?

- **When presenting to your own list** - If you're marketing to your own list, there's no need to try and entice them with a lead magnet; you've already got their contact info.

- **Product launches** - When you're trying to build momentum for a new product, a good presentation can be a lot more effective than a lead magnet on its own.

- **Joint ventures** - If someone is promoting your content to their list. We'll talk more about this in the next section of the book.

- **On your homepage** - Your teaching content should be very easy to find on your site.

Conclusion

A good lead magnet is one of the most critical elements of a successful story funnel. Don't make the mistake of thinking just because you give it away for "free" that it's an easy sell for your audience. People are very careful with whom they share their contact information and attention with these days; they're only going to convert if they see clear value in your lead magnet.

You only need one lead magnet to drive your audience to your offer successfully. Focus on creating one that successfully converts visitors and then channels the energy you would use to make others into promoting that lead magnet.

I've got a simple checklist I use when creating my lead magnets called *5 Steps To Create A Great Lead Magnet.* You can download it for yourself at resources.sellingwithstory.co.

We'll get more into promotion and driving traffic to your lead magnets and story funnel in Part III of the book.

Key Takeaways

- Lead magnets are an essential tool for collecting emails and getting people into your sales funnel.

- Make sure to use embedding within your lead magnet to show ways your audience can move forward with you.

- Keep your lead magnets short, focused on a single win, and easy to consume.

CHAPTER 12

How to Put Your Sales on Autopilot with Email Automation

A few chapters back, we explored different email automation systems. These systems are the backbone for your One Clear Path.

After a few months or years of consistent content creation, some of your best posts will be buried in the archives of your blog. Unless they generate organic search traffic, it's likely people will miss them. You can't expect a new visitor to look back through several pages in your archives to find that life-changing article you wrote last year. It's also unlikely they'll use your site's search feature to find it. Fortunately, there's a tool that can help solve this problem: the autoresponder.

An autoresponder is like having an extra member on your team. But this team member doesn't get tired of your message, take days off, or get sick.

A great series of emails will create a good experience for everyone, from your first subscriber to your millionth. In your emails, you should strive to be helpful and to anticipate the needs of the reader as well as to set their expectations for what's to come.

A well-written email will take the reader's spark of curiosity and ignite your visitor into a fan.

Sales-Based Email Automations

Lead Nurture

Your lead magnets that we discussed in the last chapter are the trigger for your lead-nurture sequences. For every lead magnet you have, you should have a sequence that follows up with the next steps on how they can go deeper on the problem. If your lead magnets are designed well and create quick wins, your audience will naturally want to take the next step with you.

A lead-nurture series is typically three to five emails long and points people to your One Clear Lesson or a low-price-point product.

A good lead-nurture series is aligned with the key desires and pain points of your audience, especially the ones your lead magnet addresses. These don't always have to be sales-based; you should also add valuable content.

Consider starting with high-value content and slowly increase the sales push over time.

- **Outline their problems -** What are the problems with your audience's current ways of doing things? Don't mention your product as the solution yet, but just help to make them aware there's some room for improvement in how they're doing things.

- **What are the benefits of working with you? -** Share some of the benefits of what taking the next step with you could look like. You've outlined the problems with what they're doing now; how does what you have help solve them? You can also consider offering some DIY solutions here that are valuable but take a lot of work. This will make what you offer look like "the easy way."

- **Overcome their laziness** - Your customers aren't really lazy, but people are often very resistant to changing their habits or the tools and systems they use. Consider what it would take to switch from what they're currently doing to what you're offering. This is really the big challenge you must overcome. Sometimes it's simply changing the way they look at things (or their mindset if you're a coach). If you're a consultant or service, it might be overcoming the "things are good enough as they are" objection. If you have software, this could be a very big challenge if they're already deeply embedded in another tool.

- **Customer success stories** - Share stories of how your customers use your product. Make sure to outline what problems it solves for them (tied to the problems outlined in the first email) and what benefits it brings them (tied to the benefits outlined in the second email). If possible, frame this email more as a how-to email to get a result or overcome a problem. Frame your customer as the hero, not yourself or your product.

- **The resources email** - The final email. Suggest some other ebooks, blogs, templates, kits, etc., for learning more about whatever it is your product does. You can also try including a discount code or special offer in this email if you haven't converted them from the previous emails; a special offer could help tip them over the edge.

Since this series is the most essential for getting your first few sales and early results, I've created a template for a starter lead-nurture series for you. You can get it at resources.sellingwithstory.co.

Upsell Series

The people who are most likely to invest in your high-ticket offers are the ones who have already invested in you. Consider creating an upsell email series that shows off your higher level products and services, outlining how the bigger investment will lead to even more value for them. Since they're already your customers, consider offering a discount or coupon to reward their commitment.

Webinar Anticipation/Replay Series

If you use webinars to sell your products, it's essential that you get as many people attending the live webinar as possible. Send them information leading up to the webinar, give them some hints at what to expect, and share good content with them (but not so much that they think they've got everything you'll cover in the webinar).

One of the biggest challenges in your sales funnel is encouraging people from registering for the webinar to actually showing up live. There's usually a huge difference in how likely your audience is to buy if they show up live versus watching a replay. Especially if there are more than a few hours between when they register and when the webinar starts. Your anticipation series is crucial for keeping interest and engagement high so more people show up live to the webinar.

As the webinar gets closer, keep your emails shorter and focus on when it's happening and what they need to know to be there.

You also want to have an email series after your webinar to let all your registrants know the replay is available. Usually, people only make replays available for a few days to encourage people to get off the fence and start consuming the content.

Consider using a variation of the lead-nurture series to follow up with anyone who attended the webinar but did not purchase from you.

Non-Sales-Based (Yet Still Essential) Email Series

Welcome Series

A welcome series is a good way to introduce yourself for the first time to new subscribers. The welcome series can set expectations for your visitors, present some of your very best content, and start conversations.

It's important that you set expectations early in this series. You want your visitors to know how many emails are coming, how often those emails will come, and what they'll contain. You want to build some anticipation and excitement for the series to keep your subscribers opening the emails.

Your visitors don't want to be blasted with emails filled with a bunch of content links. So be considerate in how you frame up your content suggestions. A good way to do this is to introduce different members of your team and have them suggest their favorite posts. This puts faces to the names of your team and casts a helpful light on your team since they're the ones suggesting the content. This also helps to make the content suggestions feel personal and unique rather than like a shameless ploy to direct traffic to your posts.

Check out these posts recommended by our team:

The Empathic Path to Inbox Zero
—*recommended by **Alex Ragsdale**, support team*

Everyone Should Feel the Customer's Pain
—*recommended by **Brett Jones**, engineering team*

How Help Scout Built a Remote Team in 6 Countries
—*recommended by **Merrill Beth Ferguson**, devops team*

Too much automation can backfire with subscribers, so you want to create opportunities for authentic interactions.

Your welcome series is a great place to collect some market research and to add a personal touch at the same time. The easiest way to do so is just through asking your audience a question:

- Why did you sign up for my product/service?

- What problem do you have that I can help with?

- What do you want to see on the blog next?

You're in :) | Plus, a quick question...

Alex from Groove
to me

Hey ▆▆,

I really appreciate you joining us at Groove, and I know you'll love it when you see how easy it is to deliver awesome, personal support to every customer.

We built Groove to help small businesses grow, and I hope that we can achieve that for you.

If you wouldn't mind, I'd love it if you answered one quick question: why did you sign up for Groove?

I'm asking because knowing what made you sign up is really helpful for us in making sure that we're delivering on what our users want. Just hit "reply" and let me know.

By the way, over the next couple of weeks, We'll be sending you a few more emails to help you get maximum value from Groove. We'll be sharing some tips, checking in with you and showing you how some of our customers use Groove to grow their businesses.

Thanks,
Alex
CEO, Groove

Product Welcome / Onboarding

Though this is not technically a sales-based series, it's indirectly essential to your sales that your customers are welcomed to the products they purchase. If you keep them engaged and successful with your products, they'll be more likely to make repeat purchases and refer others.

Don't assume they'll automatically be masters at making the most of what they just purchased. They may not even use the product at all if you don't remind them.

Depending on the product, your welcome series could provide some of the following information:

- How to get started

- Offer to book an onboarding call

- Tips and tricks to make the most of your product

- Stories of how other customers have made the most of it

If it's a digital product, you can include links and calls to action right in the emails for them to log back into the product from the email.

These are especially important if you're offering some sort of free trial. You want to ensure your customers are as successful as possible during the free trial period so it's a no-brainer when it comes time to switch over to being a paid customer. If they never spend much time engaging with your product in this period, they won't see the value in it enough to convert to a customer.

Ambassador

Most email automation software offers a *lead scoring* feature. This measures and assigns point values to actions a visitor takes (how often they open emails, click links, visit your site).

This means you can create a series for your most engaged visitors. When crafting this series, I recommend a mix of asking the audience questions about what their current problems are and what they want to see on the blog next, as well as giving them opportunities to promote some of your best content.

If you have an affiliate program, you should suggest it to this group; this will help incentivize their evangelism. Or you could request testimonials from active clients who seem to be enjoying your product. The ambassador series should make your most engaged visitors feel heard and appreciated.

Affiliate Training

If you recruit affiliates, you want to prepare them to succeed in promoting your product, just like you want to prepare your customers to succeed with your products. Preparing your affiliates to promote for you is a key part of Joint Ventures, a topic we'll discuss in the next section of the book.

Affiliate programs are a powerful way to enlist other people and brands to help grow your business. Most businesses approach this strategy by simply providing a link to their affiliates and leaving the rest up to the affiliate. You can use an email sequence to brief a new affiliate and to help them succeed. Here are a few things you could give them:

- Swipe files for email series, social media posts, and video scripts to help them sell the product.

- Information on your audience and best customers so they know who to market to.

- Great content from your blog/podcast/video channel they can share.

Resubscribe / Expiration

Remember that it's much easier to keep an existing customer rather than acquiring a new customer. So make sure you have a sales series that works to keep your customers. Most email automation tools can trigger emails based on behaviors, or what people are not doing. So you can set up a sequence that goes out only if someone has not opened an email from you or visited your website in 30 days.

If you offer a product that expires after a certain amount of time and does not automatically renew, consider making a series that reminds your customers their product is expiring and how to renew. This will rescue a lot of potentially lost customers.

This is also a good strategy if you have a membership or any program that charges a recurring fee to be a part of. If people stop engaging, they'll cancel. So make sure you're reminding them to get back into your product and experience the value you're offering.

Five Tactics for Email Automation Success

Because there are so many kinds of email programs out there, it is hard to get too specific on the features and advantages of each program. But there are many universal tactics you can apply to almost any tool you use.

1 - Be Careful Not to Bury Your Customer in Emails

If you have more than one sequence active on an individual, it's possible you are sending them too many emails and frustrating them. This can also trigger spam filters. Most email automation systems have ways to prioritize sequences so this does not happen. Be sure to ask your customer support or do research on how to do this when setting up your automations.

I've made this mistake before. I had an automation sending out daily emails for 10 days, plus I had a weekly newsletter. The emails were all high-value content, but it was too much for most people to process or enjoy. I had several complaints roll in from people who felt they were being fire-hosed with information. So I dialed my system back to only email every two to three days and skip the weekends.

2 - Come Up with a Scoring System

Most email automation platforms have a scoring system. Every opened email, link clicked, page visited, has a point value that adds into someone's *lead score*. It's up to you to determine the point values of different interactions. This can be digital body language like:

- How many emails they open

- Links they click

- Downloading content

- Registering for webinars

- Visiting certain pages on your website

Once a customer or visitor reaches certain scores, you can trigger different interactions like offering a coupon, notifying a member of your sales team that this person is highly engaged, or that someone has not used your product for a while.

Take a look at a simple spreadsheet SnapApp uses for behavioral lead scoring.

Marketing Channel	Behavior	Score
Email	Opened Email	Influencing factor (+1)
	Click within Email	Most important factor (+5)
	Forwarded Email	Influencing factor (+3)
	Unsubscribed	Negative factor (-5)
Website	Requested a Demo	Most important factor (+50)
	Visited Pricing Page	Important factor (+20)
	Visited Multiple Pages	Influencing factor (+10)
	Visited Careers Page	Negative factor (-5)
Webinar	Registered for Webinar	Influencing factor (+10)
	Attended Webinar	Important factor (+20)
Event	Attended Event	Influencing factor (+3)
	Had a good conversation	Influencing factor (+10)
	Had an amazing conversation	Important factor (+30)
Content	Downloaded White Paper	Influencing factor (+10)
	Downloaded a specific white paper	Important factor (+30)
	Completed a piece of interactive content	Influencing factor (+10)

Image source: SnapApp

3 - Surprise Them

Sometimes it's nice to throw an unexpected bonus gift into your series. Give your readers something that will delight them, something that's relevant to whatever they opted in for or purchased. This is great if you have information like their birth dates.

You want your readers to feel happy they took action and to inspire more of the same. This is true even if they have not made a purchase with you yet.

4 - Optimize for Sharing

Help your readers promote the content or products. You can make it easy by adding "click to tweet" (http://clicktotweet.com/) links inside your emails.

You must also anticipate that some of your readers will forward your emails to friends and colleagues. Make it easy for this new recipient to opt in to the sequence as well. This is usually done by adding a little "P.S." at the end of your email like:

"Did you get this email from a friend? You can get the rest of this series on X by clicking here."

5 - Don't Stop at the Sale

Create email sequences specifically for your current customers as well. Set these series up to help your customers succeed with your product, to look for opportunities to upsell, and to gather intelligence that you can apply to your prospective clients.

A great example of this comes from Yuri Elkaim at Healthpreneur group. He has follow-up emails with case studies of successful clients to inspire new clients to dive into the content they've purchased. He also provides links to the training portal, Facebook group, and other resources they've purchased, so they can dive back in and take steps to become the next great case study.

So, he went through our Health Business Accelerator workshop to have us help him roll out his online coaching program and...

Within just 7 days he had already enrolled his first high paying client ($3k price point).

Here's what he posted in our Facebook group...

 Dan
19 hrs ···

Just got my first client using the conversational close method.
I whatsapp'd a few of my old clients and one of them bit 😣
Webinar is recorded and getting ready to put it on Everwebinar today.
Boom.

The best part is that he used one of the strategies we give you called "conversational closing" that allows you to enroll clients almost immediately...without running FB ads or even having your webinar ready to go.

Conclusion

Email is one of the most powerful and easy-to-scale tools available to you. Paired with a deep understanding of your customer and audience, it can become one of the most valuable assets in your business.

A word of warning: You will not be able to completely remove yourself from email with automation without some drawbacks. You should be making an effort to personally connect with customers or your automation will come across as stale, and you will lose touch with your audience.

I have a starter template available for your lead-nurture campaign. You can download it at resources.sellingwithstory.co.

PART III

One Clear Offer

Two weeks before the money runs out . . .

Dan Norris had tried it all. After entrepreneuring for seven years, he had a lot of experience running a web design agency, creating analytics software, and thousands of other ideas in-between, but still struggled to create a successful business.

He managed to sell his agency and buy himself two years to build an incredible product. Which he channeled into the software startup, Informly.

Informly checked all the boxes of what a great "lean startup" product should look like. It was a sexy, high-tech software product. Dan had built a following with content marketing, had lots of happy beta testers using his product for free. He spent his first year developing a great product and honing the design, setting up the perfect payment gateway, and gathering feedback from influencers.

But when it came time to launch, the free users didn't convert to paid, and despite showing promise as a lean startup, it only managed to create a small trickle of revenue. After a year of desperately trying to get the product off the ground, he had come to the end of his financial runway.

With his last two weeks, he needed a new plan. He ditched trying to make Informly work and set out to develop a product that could get results fast. No sexy software, no permission from influencers, no free test users.

He created a service that would provide unlimited small WordPress fixes for a monthly fee. On Saturday he bought his domain, Tuesday the site was live, and Wednesday he sent out an email promoting the service resulting in his first paying customer. Within a week, he had 10 paying customers and was making as much as Informly was after a year.

This startup was called WP Curve, all built around the simple product of WordPress fixes. Over the course of three years, he scaled the business to a seven-figure annual recurring revenue and sold the business to GoDaddy for multiple seven figures.

Your Business is Only as Good as Your Product

It all comes down to a good product. Sales and marketing skills don't matter if you're not selling something that makes an impact. Like WP Curve, your business should be built around a great product and offer.

But there's a catch. Yes, your business should have a great product, but you should not spend a lot of time and money developing something if you're just getting started. You're not really learning about what your audience wants until you're making offers.

Dan's story is filled with lessons of what a successful product and offer can look like:

- **Get your product to market fast** - Once you've got something to offer (and you start offering it), then you start learning.

- **Keep it simple** - Start with something you can offer right away without a lot of development. Services like coaching and consulting are a good place to start.

- **You can improve as you go** - Just launch and get your product out in front of buyers. Get some customers to learn from and some cash flow to start building out your business.

What to Expect in This Section

It's beyond the scope of this book to take a deep dive into product development. A successful product in one market may flop in another market. So instead of focusing on the details of the development, we'll focus on strategies for how to get your offer in front of people.

Through this section of the book, we'll explore the assorted strategies you can use to get your offer in front of people. There are options for you whether you're mathematically minded, you like creating, or if you're a people person. It's best to pick one offer strategy to optimize and master rather than working with several.

CHAPTER 13

How to Create and Test Products Quickly

Every business starts with an idea. Many would-be entrepreneurs imagine coming up with an idea for a business with a sudden flash of clarity. It's like the story of Isaac Newton sitting under an apple tree and getting hit in the head with an apple. All of a sudden, he understands how the moon orbits the earth and has a mathematical formula to prove it. That is rarely, if ever, the case with good ideas, especially good business ideas.

The big challenge is taking an unformed, blurry idea and honing it into a product that can be shipped and that people want to pay for. But if you don't have this, you don't have a business.

The good news is there are many proven and well-developed paths to take you from idea to product. The goal of this book is to get you results fast, so I'm going to focus on a framework that will get you a shippable product as fast as possible.

In this chapter, we'll explore some strategies to get you something to sell for your business fast. If you already have a product for your business, this could help you develop your next product quickly and create something that serves your goals.

The 8 Steps of the Open Loop Product Development Framework:

The Open Loop Product Development Framework was developed by Tom Morkes and outlined in detail in his book, *Collaborate*. It combines the clarity of the Lean Startup methodology with the hands-on experimentation of Dan Norris' *7 Day Startup*. The beauty of this is it only takes a couple of days of committed focus to transform an idea to a product.

Step 1: Identify the first 10 or 100 people you want to serve. (Refer to the chapter on customer avatars for more depth on this.)

Step 2: Determine if the problem is real. Is this a problem they would really pay to have solved? Surveys and phone calls can help with this, but actions speak louder than words. Would they put money down before it's even fully developed?

Step 3: Refine and define the solution. Finding an audience and a problem they would pay to have solved is half the battle. Now you must look for a way to solve the problem with your current skills and resources. (If you can solve it first by doing work yourself, start there; don't take out a loan to develop an app yet.)

Step 4: Define your unfair advantage. Why should we pay attention to you? What makes it impossible for someone to copy what you're doing?

Step 5: Identify how you will reach your first 10/100 customers. We'll talk about some ways to do this in the next section of the book.

Step 6: Determine revenue and expenses. (How much do you plan to make from this? Is it worth your time and effort?)

Step 7: Set a ship/launch date.

Step 8: Go back through steps 1–6 several times before the vision is refined (don't take longer than a couple days), then start building your product/service/offer.

Sure, some products take much longer to develop, but consider that you don't need a fully developed product in order to sell it. If you go through the steps in this process, you can identify a need and test the market to see if people will buy it, even before you've put the effort into fully developing the product.

This is a process commonly seen in crowdfunding campaigns for physical products, but you can pre-sell courses, coaching programs, workshops, and software with the same approach.

Common Products for Online Businesses

Before we go into some specific examples, you want to consider what kind of revenue this product will bring in, as it will have a large impact on your business model.

Low Ticket - These are products that usually cost less than $300 or so. People don't need to spend a lot of time and energy thinking about whether to buy this kind of product or not. These are common in Business to Consumer (B2C) businesses. They tend to have lower margins and you'll need to sell a lot of these to succeed.

High Ticket - These products can range from $1,000 to tens of thousands, depending on the customer and the value you can provide. This is common in Business to Business (B2B) models. You usually have very high margins on these and only need to sell a few, but the sales cycle tends to be longer and much more challenging.

Recurring - This is a product people pay for repeatedly every month, quarter, or maybe each year. These products are nice because you don't always need to be hunting for new sales. You can create a nice snowball effect on your revenue over time. This works in both B2B and B2C businesses.

Now let's examine some common product types.

Courses / Information Products

Courses and other information products are some of the most common products on the market today. They're great because they're very scalable; selling one course or 1,000 courses makes a big difference in revenue, but not what's required of you in terms of fulfillment. These products can vary wildly in price depending on the perceived value and positioning.

One disadvantage with information products is they seem to be getting more and more difficult to sell. Consumers are getting more sophisticated, and they are constantly blasted with course offers. One way to counter this is to combine information products with other products listed in this chapter—like coaching or memberships—to build up perceived value.

One of the most successful information products on the market and something to aspire to create is Self-Publishing School by Chandler Bolt. This course is wildly successful, and the team at SPS is extremely good at using funnels to educate and empower its audience.

Memberships

Memberships are private, curated communities built around a certain problem or interest. These are very attractive products because they often provide recurring revenue, and highly engaged members of communities add a lot of value to your product. A good community is also one of the best places to test new product ideas.

It can be challenging to get a community to the point where it's really sustainable. They require a lot of work to maintain and keep people engaged, especially if you're charging members on a recurring basis.

A good example of a membership is James Schramko's SuperFastBusiness Community.

Coaching

This is probably one of the easiest and fastest products you can take to the market. You don't need anything more than a phone or a Skype account to get started. It's possible to do coaching one on one, or in group formats. Coaching tends to be highly profitable (if you find an audience that will pay well for the solution you provide), and it is often a recurring revenue. A few good clients can sustain a business with plenty of extra time left in your day.

A disadvantage with coaching is you're trading time for money; you only have so many hours in a day and that limits how much you can scale your business. Also, don't assume that coaching starts and stops only when you're on the phone with your clients. Coaching is an involved and demanding practice that requires you to put a lot of energy into your clients.

A great example of a unique and powerful coaching program is Kate Galliett's *The Unbreakable Body*. She provides fitness and mobility coaching with a combination of assessments, video content, and personalized one-on-one coaching. This enabled her to transition out of a brick-and-mortar gym to serve clients all around the world.

Services / Productized Services

Service businesses are a simple and reliable model. You provide a skill in exchange for a fee. These are common in B2B models. Services are the backbone of many business models and can often be brought to market quickly. You can charge as much as you want (provided you create more value than what you charge).

Often big challenges with this kind of model (especially in the early stages of business) are determining the proper price for your service. Another common challenge is setting clear expectations and limits for the service.

Productized services are a small variant on service businesses. They have clearly defined boundaries and set prices for the service they provide. Productized service models tend to eliminate much of the disadvantages of service businesses.

A great example of a productized service is Meryl Johnston's Bean Ninjas, which provides bookkeeping for a monthly fee. They only work in Xero and have several clear and well-defined plans which makes their business very scalable.

Live Events / Workshops

Don't think that just because a majority of your business runs online means you're restricted to only online products. Hosting live workshops is a powerful way to create a lot of revenue in a short time for your business. A workshop typically hosts between five and 20 people, depending on your capacity, and live events like seminars can host many more.

The big challenge with events is there are a lot of risks assumed in reserving a space and all the details associated with it. It's also a lot of work to get people in the seats.

One of the most successful workshops out there is the Stage Execution Workshop by Advance Your Reach. People attend this two-day workshop and leave with a system to help them predictably get speaking gigs.

Affiliate

You may not even need a product at all if you have a strong audience. You can sell other people's products and take a commission for it. This means you have very little risk or overhead for your business. This is also a good way to see what products are successful and get a good idea of what the market wants so you can develop a product of your own in the future.

The problem with this model is you need a massive following to make it sustainable. Your margins are very small since you're not selling your own products, and you lack a certain degree of control over what you earn.

Conclusion

Without a good product, you don't have a business. But following the Open Loop Product Development Framework and choosing a good product type should help you get to market quickly. The sooner you start selling and growing your business, the more opportunities will come your way.

Remember that you don't need to have a fully developed product in order to start selling it. Start testing your ideas by making offers and seeing if you can get your customers to pay you to develop it.

Key Takeaways

- It's better to build products quickly and test them in the market, rather than spending a lot of time and money developing something.

- Follow the Open Loop Framework to quickly build and test your products.

- When choosing a product, make sure the product model fits your goals.

CHAPTER 14

Pitching Your Product

The end goal of creating a funnel is to sell your product. This system is all about making it simple to create revenue for your business. Sales and revenue hinge on how well you can pitch your product and how open the audience is to the pitch. You can't just say, "Buy this thing," and expect people to pull out their credit cards. This is a subtle and intricate process that will call upon all the storytelling skills we've been developing throughout this book.

Depending on the price of your product, and the mindset of the audience, the audience members may require some extra help to get them to pull the trigger. Even with low-priced products that are sold in e-commerce stores, getting someone to switch what they buy or change a behavior may take some convincing.

In this chapter, we're going to look at a few strategies for product pitching to get you started on your sales. Depending on what you are selling, some of these may work better for you than others, so keep an open mind and experiment.

Direct Pitch vs. Strategy Session

Depending on what you're selling, you may want to consider offering a strategy session, instead of just directly pitching your product. If you're offering a counseling service, a coaching program, or anything that's selling yourself and your team instead of an actual product, a strategy session may be a good idea.

A strategy session allows you to speak one on one with the potential customer and allows you to really identify their specific needs and frame your offering in just the language they need to hear. It's easier to get people to commit to a strategy session than buying the product outright.

Most people online are savvy enough these days to know that a "strategy session" or "free consultation" is often just a sales call in disguise. So you want to frame and name your session in a way that speaks to the value they're getting. Think about how you can create a Grandma's Lasagna process for your strategy sessions. How can you name your strategy session in a way that focuses on results and builds desire for it?

A financial planner might have a "cash flow recovery assessment."
A business coach might have a "hidden opportunity discovery session."
A chiropractor might have a "mobility assessment."

Qualification

If you've set up your full One Clear Path, someone will need to jump through several hoops (downloading content, watching a full challenge or a webinar and booking a call) to end up on the phone with you. So they're typically well-qualified for what you're offering.

Nevertheless, you may want to add friction to the process, especially if you've got a high-ticket offer that's going to require a lot of your time and energy. There's nothing worse than getting into a project and realizing it's not a good fit. You've wasted time and energy, neither you nor the customer feels good about it, and they're not likely to recommend you to others after this.

So adding another step in this process and having an application for your strategy calls may be a good move. Ask questions that could help you determine whether they're a good fit or not. Are they willing to invest what it takes? Do they have the capacity to do their parts? This can help you screen potential customers who aren't a good fit for you. Plus, this extra friction often increases the desire for what you're offering.

If you want to add even more friction, you can have an application fee for your strategy calls. The small investment ensures that only the most engaged people will book calls with you. I recommend making this fee refundable if you speak with them and they're not a good fit, only keep the fee if they end up being a "no show."

Sales Pages / Sales Letters

Sales letters have been in use since the beginning of direct response advertising in the early 20th century. They're the ultimate test of your skills in writing good copy that speaks to the heart of your audience.

The length of your sales page will largely be determined by the price of the product and how much nurturing you've done before they arrive on the page. The higher the price of the product you're selling, the longer the page should be.

Here are a few key elements to every good sales page:

- An attention-grabbing headline that speaks to the desire or pain your audience is feeling.

- Text and images that clearly point out who this product is and is not for.

- Copy that presents the problem and then steps them into their "dream situation" with their problem solved and desires fulfilled.

- Clearly established authority with testimonials, data, press logos.

- A clear explanation of what they get if they buy and how this solves their problems.

- A clear call to action.

There's more to great sales pages; people dedicate their whole careers to writing these well. If you want to start getting results fast, check out the chapter on design hacking to learn how you can start building these pages quickly.

Video Sales Letters

Video sales letters work the same as a sales page, but instead of writing only, the message is delivered over video. This can be more effective for some types of audiences and especially mobile users. They can allow for a little more flexibility by leveraging visual storytelling over language, but make sure you're getting your message right.

I recommend having a video sales letter on your sales page right at the top, giving your audience the choice to consume your message over video or by reading.

Email Pitch

It's rare to only pitch a product in an email itself. Using your email sequences to remind your audience about the offers after your webinar, and to try to get them off the fence, is a good use for email when it comes to product pitches.

You can use much of the copy you create outlining the pain and benefits of what you're offering for your landing pages in your email sequences. Leverage the timing of your automations to reinforce the urgency of your offer. If you're only offering your product for a few days after the webinar, then remind them that time is running out in your sequences.

Conclusion

Many entrepreneurs dread the pitch. I get it, most of you are probably not natural marketers or salespeople. You've spent years honing your skills to help people, and you'd probably rather just do that and not have to deal with this stuff. If this sounds like you, I want to invite you to change your perspective, if only for a moment.

You have something valuable that the world needs, and it's your responsibility to help people with it. Selling is a service to them. Through your sales, you're communicating that you believe in the person and their ability to improve their lives or their businesses. You're working to overcome whatever is holding them back from becoming a better version of themselves. Money is not the issue—it's never the issue. So stand strong in your offering and take ownership of your sales. It will change the way you show up in your strategy calls, webinars, and copy.

Key Takeaways

- It's often better for high-ticket products to offer a strategy session to get some time to speak one on one before offering your product.

- In some cases, you may want to have an application to qualify your audience before offering the product to them.

- Use several pitching strategies (emails, sales pages, and presentations) to follow up with your prospects.

CHAPTER 15

Fast-Track Your Sales and List Growth with Joint Ventures

If you're just starting out, you probably don't have a big list to sell to. This is certainly something you want to build in the long run, but there are many strategies you can leverage to get some sales now and accelerate your list growth.

One of my favorites is a Joint Venture or JV. A JV is two or more people coordinating a promotion together and splitting the profits. Most commonly, this means one person has a product and a high-quality, educational presentation, and another has a list of engaged people who could benefit from the message and product. The person with the list invites their audience to a free training; the content provider gives the presentation, and at the end, presents a way to move deeper. The revenue from the sales gets split between the host and the content provider.

The real benefit of joint venture webinars, however, is that they are the fastest way to grow your list with no upfront cost. You can add people by the hundreds or thousands. You only pay commissions on products when they're sold. This differs from advertising platforms like Facebook, where you pay for ads whether they result in sales or not. This means there is essentially no financial risk for companies as they look to build their audiences.

In addition, when you mail to your own list, you can only offer a product a few times a year to that same list before your audience begins to get burned out. Joint venture marketing provides you with brand-new audiences and lists, so you can promote your product more often without having to worry about extra costs. Plus, you can offer your own growing audience new things that complement your primary product—without spending days or weeks creating a new product yourself.

Finding Influencers to Partner With

The most ideal people to partner with are those who serve the same audience that you have defined in your *customer avatar* (mentioned in Part I of this book). Get creative in imagining the different ways people provide complimentary services to your audience. If you sell a product about dieting, it's likely an audience interested in other health topics like posture or sleep could be receptive to your message.

Go to where your ideal audience spends time and gathers information. There are plenty of digital platforms on which you can build relationships with experienced people in your field. Look in Facebook or LinkedIn groups, or on question sites like Quora and find people who are sharing valuable content. Also, make an effort to attend offline events, seminars, and meetups. Look for people who are traveling around and being the movers and shakers in your industry.

There are lots of different ways you can spot an influencer with a big following:

- Their posts on social media get big engagement.

- The talks they give are highly anticipated and they fill the room.

- Other people are mentioning them and talking about them.

- Their books, podcasts, or video channels have lots of good reviews and subscribers.

Start Building Relationships

Once you spot an influencer, don't just start firing off your idea to do a joint venture with them. Too often we approach influencers with this "take value" mentality and fall back on our worst behavior.

We become so fixated on how someone could help us that we forget to consider how we could help them. I call this the *reverse value trap*. Once we're caught in this trap, we go around asking for things from people who don't know us or trust us without presenting anything we can offer in return. Almost everyone gets caught in this trap at some point; some learn to avoid it, while most of us get perpetually stuck in it.

Put yourself in the shoes of the people you want to reach out to. Anyone with even a small degree of visibility and authority gets their inboxes flooded every day with people who are caught in the reverse value trap. Here's what it looks like from their side:

- Someone asking to pick your brain about a half-baked business idea.

- Getting asked to add barely relevant links to your best articles.

- Getting asked to send out an offer to your list for a dubious product.

Always stay focused on how you can add value to them first. To do this, find ways you can be a genuine help to the people you want to connect with. Don't worry about getting compensated for the value you add. You should trust that the rewards for building this relationship will come in the future and remember that they may not come in the form of something you're expecting or are even aware of right now.

- **Provide Your Skills -** Are you a great designer or good with audio? Maybe you have some coding or tech skills? See if there's a way you can offer your talents to them.

- **Engage With and Promote Their Content** - Pretty simple, right? Just follow them on social media and start commenting on and promoting their content. Your engagement should aim to spark conversation. Ask open-ended questions, or point out ideas that resonate with you.

- **Help Their Audience -** Sometimes it's difficult to add value directly to an influencer, but you can still help them by adding value to their audience. If they have a Facebook Group or an online community, go above and beyond adding value there.

- **Be Their "Poster Child" -** Find an article or guide created by the person you want to reach out to that would be valuable to apply to your own business. Then follow it to the T, work hard to implement the systems they recommend, and take careful notes on what you do and the results you get. Then make a case study outlining what you did and the results you got. With this content, you've become an amazing testimonial to that person. This will both flatter and interest the person you reach out to.

Be patient and generous in this process; it could take months or more to build the trust and rapport to the point where they're open to a JV. Find value in the relationship beyond the JV potential so you can enjoy this partnership you are creating.

Leverage Introductions

Getting introduced to an influencer by someone they already trust is one of the fastest ways to create trust in yourself.

Many entrepreneurs don't fully leverage the power of the connections they already have for introductions. This is one of your most powerful untapped resources.

LinkedIn is a particularly good resource to discover mutual connections. Once you identify an influencer you want to collaborate with on a JV, look at the mutual connections you have with them.

The Core Elements of Joint Ventures

Once you've found a partner to do a JV with, the fun really starts to happen. There are a few things you need to get clear on before running the joint venture, however. You need to get clear on a few key elements of your JV before the promoting and presenting starts.

The Negotiation

The foundation of a JV is understanding the promotion strategy. Sometimes one person is promoting, and the other is providing the product. Sometimes you're cross-promoting each other's products. You'll also want to get clear on how you will split the sales. In the case of information products, it's common for 40–60% to go to the list owner. But if you have a service or something with more overhead, you'll want to find an agreement that won't undercut your margins. There's a careful balance here; if you offer too little to the list owner, they may not let you present.

Once you have agreed on what your partnership will look like, you will pick a date for the promotion and create a promotion schedule. When will the emails be going out? What will the character of the campaign be? As a presenter, you're going to want to get some firm and clear commitments from the list owner here. They tend to under-promote if their commitments are unclear.

The Promotion

Based on your discussions with your partner, you can begin building the back-end of the promotion. This means scheduling a webinar, building a landing page that has the functionality to get visitor emails, and building a JV kit. This kit should contain email swipes, a link to a registration page, a summary of your promotion, and affiliate links.

Make the process as simple as possible for them. This will make it more likely that they will continue to partner with you in the future if you have promotions that would benefit from a joint venture.

As part of your promotion, you should develop both the main offer and a downsell offer for those who do not purchase the main one. Determine how long each of these offers will run. The downsell can essentially be a discount version of the main offer, just missing some bells and whistles that are included in that main promotion.

At this point, you'll want to triple-check that all your links, emails, and promotional materials are set up properly. A faulty webinar registration link or some other minor tech mishap can really hurt your profits.

The Presentation

With your agreement in place and promotions sent out, you're all set to give your presentation. Draw upon everything you've learned from the storytelling and teaching strategies we've discussed to share powerful content with the audience.

There are some cases where no presentation is necessary and all the list host does is promote a lead magnet, product, or service through email. These promotions are better for low-ticket products that don't need much convincing to purchase.

After the Joint Venture

If you get someone's information and collaborate with them, set reminders for yourself to follow up with them and keep touching base. You will completely stand out by being the person who actually followed through. This is essential whether you're following up after meeting someone at an event or you collaborated on content.

It's just as important after you have run a promotion together to do a follow-up debrief. You can find out what the partner did and did not like, so you can set yourself up for success in potential future partnerships.

By being proactive about following up with your partner after a promotion, not only do you keep the relationship open for another potential partnership down the road, but you also open up possibilities for your partner to make new introductions to other potential partners. In this way, a successful joint venture can lead to new business opportunities down the road.

Conclusion

If there's one skill that can have an outsized impact on your business (and life outside of business), it's relationship-building. Think back to one of the big turning points of your life—that first customer, that new job, closing that deal—it probably happened as a result of a relationship you built.

Joint ventures are extremely powerful to leverage relationships for fast list growth and sales. Don't just rely on building your own social media following or organic SEO traffic to start selling your product. Remember to focus on adding value first when building relationships and coordinating joint ventures. Through true connections based on trust and value, you can open doors to grow your brand (and your bank account) sustainably.

Key Takeaways

- Successful joint ventures are built on the foundations of strong relationships. Strive to add value and build trust with potential partners before proposing a JV.

- Make sure you're very clear about what everyone's commitments are, especially with promotions.

- The fortune is in the follow-up. If you get a "no," keep in touch with the person and maybe another opportunity with happen. Even if you get a "yes," stay in touch and keep the relationship warm after the JV to keep the door open for more opportunities.

CHAPTER 16

Scalable Marketing for Storytellers

With a good product, an automated system to tell people about the product, and a strong message that resonates with those who need the product in place, your job becomes simple: get your message in front of as many people who resonate with it as possible. While there are many ways to do this, and we'll explore several approaches, I believe that building a solid foundation on a scalable platform is an essential foundation in this day and age.

There are many ways to build a scalable marketing platform that will help you build your following and get more attention to your product and message. Basically, they all boil down to one thing: great content. By content, I don't just mean blogging. The ideas in this chapter can apply to podcasting, video, and any social media platform.

While sending your message out across these platforms is not always directly related to your sales, you use these tools to build a relationship with your audience and keep yourself at the top of their minds. It does not cost much to get started on any of these platforms. With the right strategy, you can grow your reach from hundreds to hundreds of thousands.

The reality is each of the platforms and the skill sets associated with them deserve their own books (There are countless books dedicated to each.). It's beyond the scope of this book to go in-depth on anything mentioned in this chapter, so instead of discussing the different platforms at length, we'll explore a philosophy to approach any of them.

Why Content?

Content marketing is the foundational way to connect with your audience online. But unlike many of the other tools and strategies we've discussed in this book, it's not easy to track or predict. That's why it's important to have your sales system dialed in before you really start investing in content; you don't want to create from a place of neediness. People are very sensitive to needy marketers and will turn away at the first sign.

Successful content is based on generosity and authenticity. Focus on solving the problems and meeting the needs of your audience. We've already done a lot of the work in researching their problems and mindsets in earlier chapters; you can put that information to good use in your content here as well.

It's important to know that your ideal customers are not evenly distributed across all stages of the Buyer's Journey. It's likely a majority of your audience (up to 80%) are in the Know phase; most of them aren't ready to make a move. Once they move into the Like and Trust phases, it could be a matter of weeks, days, or sometimes hours before they make a purchase.

Creating good content your audience members can consume for free will help you build a relationship with them and stay at the forefront of their minds when the time comes for them to take the next step.

There's More to Content Than Customers

Great content will reward you with more than just customers. Many of the people you connect with may never purchase from you, but they can still add a tremendous amount of value to you.

To this end, consider the value of:

- a follower who is not an "ideal customer," but who is a raving fan who promotes your content to others.

- a new team member who is inspired by your beliefs and vision.

- meeting future strategic partners who are inspired to collaborate with you through content.

- a new investor in your business who appreciates the quality of the content you create.

SEO Content vs. Social Content

There are two basic approaches to creating content. Both are valid; they each offer a few benefits and drawbacks.

SEO Content

SEO content is a classic approach to content marketing. You're creating content to appear in search engines. This is great because if you succeed, it delivers consistent month-over-month traffic. This is especially good if you can rank for a keyword that people search for when they're ready to make a purchase.

Let's imagine you help people with product launches. "Ways to make money online" is a long-tail keyword with lots of competition and searches, and it does have a slight problem-solving intent, but it would not be a good keyword for your business. Compare that with the search keyword phrase "product launch plan template," which gets much fewer searches, but has less competition and is laser-focused on a problem you can solve. In the end, this keyword phrase will be more effective at driving lucrative traffic to your site.

Unfortunately, the world of SEO has become extremely competitive, and most industries and niches require a tremendous amount of investment to succeed. Plus, if you're just starting out, it can take a long time (6–12 months) to really see results, another reason you don't want to rely on content to drive your sales.

Contagious Content

Contagious content is an approach I think many of the readers of this book will fare better with. Instead of focusing on keywords, focus on your beliefs and your story. You still want to create content that, for the most part, relates to the key problems and goals your audience has. But instead of just solving the problem with another how-to video or article, add in your own philosophy, experience, or beliefs.

I mean really, when someone has the "101 Uses For Coconut Oil" article written, what are you going to do? Write "131 Uses For Coconut Oil That You've Never Seen!"? Well, you could. Or you could do a live video where you go on a rant about why you think the world has gone crazy over coconut oil. Those who share your point of view will like you and trust you more after seeing your contagious content.

Sharing your beliefs, especially when they're polarizing, is what will stand out in the noisy world of content and connect with those who share your beliefs. Yes, you risk driving some people away, but do you even want to work with people who don't resonate with you?

There's another careful balance here; you don't want to share any polarizing idea just for the sake of attention. It must be something you care about and should also be able to relate back to your story and the audience's needs.

Conclusion - It's Better to be Different Than Better

It's beyond the scope of this book to figure out the best content marketing strategy for you. Do you choose video or written? Instagram or Facebook? It's hard to tell; plus the landscape is constantly changing, and what works this year may not work next year.

What's timeless is your story and authenticity and the connections it can create. The more of you that you can mix into your content and message, the easier it will be to reach the people who want to hear it.

So consider how you can be different in the marketplace, your personality quirks, what you stand for and against, and your unique perspective are all powerful tools to connect with content.

Key Takeaways

- Identify one medium (audio, video, written) and one channel (blogs, YouTube, Instagram) to share your content. Mastering a single channel is better than being mediocre in many.

- Make sure to have your One Clear Path to Sales system in place and working before you start creating lots of content.

- Use your content as a tool not only to build a relationship with your audience, but also to build relationships with other influences to create JV opportunities.

CHAPTER 17

What You Need to Know to Succeed With Paid Traffic

Paid traffic is one of the most desired marketing channels in the online space. In many ways people see it like a faucet; turn it on and money comes out, turn it up and more money comes out! Great, right?

This is possible and achievable for anyone with a modest budget, moderate technical abilities, and an attitude that's open to experimentation. With a sales funnel that's converting reliably and some well-targeted ads, you can have a powerful system to create new sales whenever you need them. It's pretty magical having the confidence you can always create new revenue when you need it.

While that can be the case sometimes, if you're unprepared for paid traffic, you'll just bleed out your hard-earned cash with no result.

To succeed with paid traffic, you need a lot of clarity into how your audience is engaging with your funnel.

It's beyond the scope of this book to teach you everything about paid traffic. But I can help prepare you with the right questions to ask and give you a strategy to get you ready for paid traffic.

Before You Start With Paid Traffic

Paid traffic is not always a good investment. It often requires some experimentation, and thus mistakes, to be run profitably. You need to have a few things in place to make the most of your investment in paid traffic.

Below are some minimum requirements I would recommend having in place before you begin a lightweight campaign like the ones outlined in this chapter. As the amount of money you use in your paid traffic goes up, so should the sophistication of your tracking and automation.

Your Funnel Needs to be in Place

Collecting a bunch of leads won't do you much good if you don't have your funnel developed. This, at a minimum, means you need a lead magnet and a core offer in place.

If you just want to collect leads to build an audience, it's probably better to invest your ad budget in creating good content on your site.

You Need Analytics

You need some visibility into how people are behaving on your site and in your funnel. Good analytics tools can show you where your funnel is working well and where there may be "leaks" in your funnel. It can show you where people are spending the most time and are the most engaged with your content and where people may be dropping off.

Many of the tools I recommended for email automation and landing pages do have analytics built into their systems. But you'll need to collect data from several locations to do this.

Analytics tools can help you answer the following questions:

- Are people opening and clicking through on the emails I've sent them?

- Are my landing pages converting?

- I'm testing two different versions of a landing page, which is converting better?

- Are people watching my webinars all the way through? Or when do they drop off?

- Who is referring traffic to me?

You Need Your Pixels

Many analytics platforms use something called a pixel to collect data. A pixel is a snippet of code you paste on your website that gathers information about your visitors.

As of the writing of this book, the most popular platforms for ads are Facebook and Instagram. One of the easiest and best things you can do right away is to set up a Facebook Business account and get a pixel installed on your website to start collecting data.

Even if you think you're a long way off from running ads yourself, having this data gives you insights into who is visiting your page and empowers you to start running ads whenever you want. It can take up to 90 days to really collect enough data to run retargeting ads, so if you wait until you think you're "ready" to install your pixel then you're stuck.

Installing a pixel sounds complicated, but it really is usually just a matter of copy and paste. You can find your pixel code in the Facebook Business Manager. Your landing page tools will often have a clear place to paste this snippet, and you can easily install a WordPress plugin for a Facebook pixel.

Start With Small Experiments

It can be intimidating to approach paid traffic if you don't know what these numbers are for your own business. At the beginning of your product launch you won't know any of them. It's still a good idea to experiment and start collecting this information with paid traffic. You just don't want to take out a loan and start spending thousands each day on Facebook.

Start with a small budget and carefully monitor how people respond to your ads. Get clear on how you're tracking your numbers and what you need to look for during these experimental phases.

As you begin to dial in your ads by targeting and messaging, you can slowly up your budget. Over time, you'll develop a level of clarity around how well your system is performing and have the confidence that if you invest a dollar in ads, you'll make two, five, or ten more in return.

The Goal of an Ad

One of the most common mistakes people make on ads is they try to sell their full product from the ad. This can be a tough thing to do with the limited attention span you're working with. Unless you're selling a product that could be an impulse buy, it's not the best use of your money.

If we really break down the goal of an ad, there are just two simple things we need to achieve:

1. **Get attention -** You need to break through the noise and capture their attention.

2. **Get them to click the ad -** You just need to build up enough desire and interest for them to click the ad and start to learn more.

This can really simplify your ad strategy. No longer do you need to be the next David Ogilvy and write the most amazing ad to sell your high-end mastermind in a few clever words. All you need to do is just build enough interest and emotional resonance to get them to click to the landing page for your lead magnet or One Clear Lesson. Then you can let your landing page handle the work of moving them to the next step.

The Gold is in the Data

While experimenting with ads, you're collecting valuable data that you can use later. Thanks to the pixel I mentioned earlier in this chapter, every time someone clicks your ad or visits your website, you'll collect data on them that you can use later.

With Facebook and other platforms like Perfect Audience, you can use this data to get insight into who is visiting your site. With Facebook, you can see things like age, gender, and other behavioral/ demographic data. Compare this to what you've outlined in your audience avatar and see if it lines up.

You can also use this data later for retargeting. Retargeting at its core is displaying offers only to people who have connected with your content before, whether it's a video on Facebook, or a post on your website. Since they've engaged with your content before, they're more valuable and effective to target than cold traffic (those who have never seen or heard of you before).

This is great because it gives you multiple opportunities to reach and connect with your audience. It often takes several "touches" (seeing your content, ads, videos, etc.) to capture the attention and curiosity of your audience.

Scaling Up - What to Ask When Running Paid Traffic

To truly be able to use ads and scale them beyond a small budget, you need to understand a few key numbers. Being able to have clarity on the answers to the questions below will allow you to build a strong paid traffic strategy that has the best chance for profit.

How Much am I Able to Spend to get a Customer?

This question has to do with the margins on your product or service. With paid traffic, you're essentially trading your profit of what you sell for advertising. If you're spending more than the margins you're making, then you're losing money. So you need to know how much profit you're willing to give away.

Depending on what you're selling, this number could vary wildly. If you are selling a physical product, this will be the margin of the product you can spend before breaking even. For a high-ticket consulting offer, you may have a lot of margin to spend.

The more you can spend to acquire a customer, the better, so having clarity here is essential to success.

Are People Staying Engaged Through my One Clear Lesson?

Whether it's a webinar, a course, or a book, you'll want to know if your teaching content is engaging enough to keep people's attention through the whole presentation. If people aren't staying to the end when you make your call to action, then you've got a problem.

This is a sign you need to rework your teaching content. Change the format, what you teach, the "big idea" discussed in Chapter 9 on building a One Clear Lesson.

How Well Does My Funnel Convert?

Beyond your presentation, you also need to make sure people are converting on your landing pages and clicking through your email automations in your sales funnel.

If you understand how well your funnel converts, then you can have a good guess of how many leads you need to hit your target number of customers. This helps you determine when you're going to expect a return on your investment with paid traffic. If it's going to take a long time for them to convert, you may not want to sink all your cash into ads right away.

How Long Does it Take for a Lead to Become a Customer?

Depending on how your funnel and content is constructed, it may take a few days, weeks, or months for a new lead to become a customer.

Typically, with the One Clear Path strategy, you should expect most of your conversions in one or two weeks. You want to act fast with the leads to get them to move deeper with you (especially when you're using paid traffic).

For those that don't convert right away, nurture them with good content and keep yourself on their radar for when they're ready to buy.

How Much Does it Cost to Get a Lead?

This one is not really something you can figure out before you start with ads. You'll want to start with a small (maybe $5–$10 a day) budget to see how well your ads are converting and what it costs to get a new lead in your funnel.

At this point, you should experiment with a few different audiences to target and some varied designs and copy on your ads to see what's resonating.

You can hone in on your best performing ads by looking at the cost of getting a lead.

Total Leads ÷ Total Spend on Your Ads = Cost to Get a Lead

Conclusion

Paid traffic is one of the most powerful tools out there for getting traffic to your funnel. But like all powerful tools, it needs to be used intelligently to get the results you want.

I encourage you to start experimenting with it once you've got a sales funnel established. Keep an open mind and don't expect amazing results right away. Consider your early ad spending to be investing in education and experimentation. Start asking the questions and getting clear on the key metrics mentioned in this chapter and scale up slowly.

Key Takeaways

- Start with small experiments in paid traffic to get a feel for the tools before you invest heavily.

- Remember that your pixel is gathering data for you to better understand and retarget people who visit your site and sales funnel.

- Make sure you're asking the right questions and using the data you gather from your experiments to know your numbers.

CHAPTER 18

Storytelling on Stage - How To Use Speaking To Grow Your Business

Though most of this book is based around digital marketing and storytelling strategies, you also want to connect with people in offline environments. As powerful as all the digital tools that we've explored are, there's no substitute for spending real, physical time with your audience and other influencers in your space.

Speaking is powerful. Spending an hour on stage in front of the right audience can create the same connection and trust that would take months to develop online.

There are few people who know this better than Pete Vargas, who, after having his life deeply impacted by a speaker, decided to dedicate his life to helping people share their message from stages. He was his own first case study. In less than three years, he built a thriving seven-figure business almost entirely from the stage. He was brilliant at finding and landing stages, but for most of his career, he was only helping others share their message and get on stages themselves.

Starting his company, Advance Your Reach, was terrifying; his first three minutes speaking on a Bo Eason speakoff were terrifying. But with a focused and persistent strategy, he was able to hone and refine his talk into the most powerful marketing tool for his business.

I've had the honor of seeing this journey unfold for Pete. I was also impacted by seeing his message on a webinar and became a customer. I resonate with his message and goal, so I quickly offered my help in achieving his vision to impact one billion people through stages by 2027. At the time of writing this, I am a coach for his workshops and have helped hundreds of entrepreneurs, coaches, and influencers develop powerful talks and get on their dream stages.

It all started with a great talk. A 60-minute presentation that impacted me.

Perhaps your talk will not only inspire customers to join your vision, but bring you new team members as well.

Speaking Gigs are Everywhere

For most people, when thinking of a stage or speaking gig, we think of a giant, Tony Robbins motivational event with thousands of people in the audience. While events like this are memorable, there's a much bigger world out there for speaking, and much more opportunity, even if you're new to speaking.

A simple Google search of "conferences for [your target audience]" (you can try events/masterminds/meetups/associations/seminars in place of conferences, too) and you're likely to find dozens of potential events.

Associations - These are memberships for people of a certain profession or skill set. They join associations for networking and professional development opportunities. Most associations have local, state, and national chapters, each with their own events. Giving a great talk at one association's local chapter could lead to more opportunities for the state and national levels.

Seminars / Conferences - These are events open to the public. Often they're more open to allowing speakers to sell from the stage. You can find seminars of all different audience sizes and for any industry.

Meetups - If you live in or near a major city, there are countless meetups happening. Look on meetup.com to find active groups of people who are already interested and discussing topics related to your business. You can also create your own very easily.

Masterminds - Masterminds are similar to associations, but are usually a much smaller group. Though the audience size is smaller, they're usually highly curated members. Even though it's a small stage, it could be one of your most valuable.

Remember that the ideal stage is one where the audience is filled with potential buyers for your offer. Try to focus only on events that fit this profile. In the early stages of your speaking, you may take any opportunity that gives you a chance to practice, but you want to work your way toward only speaking at ideal events to make sure the time and effort you spend getting on these stages is worthwhile.

Who Controls the Stage?

The real work begins once you find a stage you want to speak on. The first step is properly identifying who is in control of the stage you want to get on.

Finding the event planner is not always easy; the event planners are not usually the keynote speakers or the big faces of the event. They typically work behind the scenes.

Look on the event page for a list of team members involved with the event. You can also check these names on LinkedIn; often they'll have a position or job description that will mention they are in charge of vetting speakers.

Here are some basic titles to get you started: director of events, director of education, director of professional development.

Simply calling the organization and asking may also be a fast route to figuring out who the event planner is. But once you know who they are, you need to be prepared with outreach.

Making a Good Impression on the Gatekeeper

Event planners are very protective of their audiences, and rightly so. For every event, they need to filter through dozens, if not hundreds, of potential speakers to find the right ones for their event. They need to be highly selective and protective because one bad speaker can sour a whole event. They're incredibly protective of their audiences and events for this reason.

In your outreach, you need to make a good impression on the event planner and start building trust from the start. Fortunately, doing this is simpler than you might think.

Solve a problem - Event planners get approached all the time with people trying to sell something. It's rare to find someone who genuinely wants to solve a problem and provide great content.

Add value first - You might be surprised at how bad most outreach to event planners really is. 99% of the messages they get are all about what they want the event planner to do for them. It's never about how they can help the planner have a better day or succeed in their goals. You're going to be different—always seek to add value.

Be patient and rebound the 'no's - You're only going to land a small fraction of stages you reach out to on the first try. A "no" now is not a "no" forever, so be gracious even when rejected, continue to add value to them, and prepare to try again for the next event. It might take years to get on some of the biggest and most valuable stages on your list, but it's worth the effort.

Get out of the email inbox - For every 100 emails an event planner gets, they probably received two phone calls and one letter in the mail. So separate yourself from the pack and get on the phone or send them something in the mail.

Be in the audience - One of the best places to start when building relationships with event planners is in the audience. Attend the events where you want to speak and get to know who is managing it.

For a bit of a deeper dive into building relationships, I recommend referring to the relationship-building strategies mentioned in the Joint Venture chapter.

Positioning Yourself as an Expert

You might be thinking, "I want to speak, but I've never spoken before and I'm not famous." I'm happy to tell you that it's possible to position yourself as an expert without being famous.

Speaker One-sheet - This is the most basic asset you need to develop. A single sheet of paper that shares your bio, the problem you solve for the audience, popular speaking topics, and some social proof. I also like creating a digital version of the one-sheet by building this information into a landing page and including videos. A good video can just be you addressing the camera for two to three minutes on why you're a great fit for the stage.

Good Video - There are two videos you'll really want to have available for an event planner. Each of these serve as an audition, so make sure you're sharing your best self. The first is a video where you just speak to the camera and say why you're a good fit for their audience. This can be a generic video, or for a really big stage, you may want to make a fully custom video that specifically mentions the event. A second important video is uncut footage of you speaking, anyone can make a fancy sizzle reel to make your talk look like the next *Star Wars* movie trailer, but a good uncut clip of you speaking really tells the truth of how you engage the audience.

The Real Purpose of a Speaking Fee

A lot of speakers get hung up on the whole idea of a speaking fee; they want to command as high a fee as possible.

You should have a speaking fee, but you should use it strategically. Don't worry about getting paid to speak, if you have a good presentation and are in front of the right audience, there's much more value on the back-end from selling your products than there is for your speaking fee.

So why should you have a fee? It's an essential bargaining chip you can use to negotiate with event planners. You can often waive your speaking fee in exchange for other benefits:

- Getting a booth at the event

- Being allowed to mention your products from the stage

- Doing a webinar for the audience before or after the event

- Giving a gift (maybe your One Clear Lesson?) to the whole list of attendees

Conclusion

The world of speaking, though not online, can be one of the most powerful marketing tools for a good storyteller. Don't be afraid to venture outside of the digital realm and start mingling with people at events like these.

All the storytelling strategies outlined earlier in this book can be just as easily applied to a good talk as a good webinar or sales video. The teaching content you put together for your One Clear Lesson can be repurposed into a talk.

Key Takeaways

- Speaking opportunities both online and offline are everywhere. Presenting is one of the fastest ways to drive growth for our business if done well.

- The key to getting speaking opportunities is to understand who the gatekeeper is and how to meet their needs.

- Remember to use your speaking fee as a negotiation tool, not as a primary source of income.

The End

Congratulations! You've made it to the end. You now have the tools and knowledge you need to build your very own One Clear Path to Sales.

Just because you've made it to the end of the book does not mean you should put it back on the shelf and forget about it. Use it as a guidebook and reference as you continue to build the different elements of your One Clear Path to Sales. Give yourself plenty of time and space to experiment with these systems. It's rare to get it all right the first time, so have an open mind and find what's working for you.

You have much more to share with the world than just a product. Your story, knowledge, and experience can impact thousands of people. You'll impact people in ways you can't anticipate. Though you've built a story so your customer is the hero, you're going to be a hero in their eyes as you start sharing your gifts and helping people.

I want to leave you with a quote to ponder by Albus Dumbledore from the *Harry Potter* books about the power of language and story:

"Differences of habit and language are nothing at all if our aims are identical and our hearts are open."

To me, this quote points out that by deliberately crafting a story for your life and your work, you can change how you show up in the world. By living a story—your story—you can live aligned with your deep purpose. Your audience will sense this and be inspired by it.

Please keep in touch and let me know how you're progressing on your own Hero's Journey. You can get in touch, check out the podcast, read more articles, and learn about my other books and services at thestoryengine.co.

Cheers,
Kyle

Made in the USA
San Bernardino, CA
08 May 2019